TWICE ON SUNDAYS

Smyth & Helwys Publishing, Inc.
6316 Peake Road
Macon, Georgia 31210-3960
1-800-747-3016
©2023 by Bill Witherington III
All rights reserved.

Library of Congress Cataloging-in-Publication Data

Names: West, James Arthur, 1895-1988, author. | Witherington, Ben, III,
 1951- editor, writer of added commentary.
Title: Twice on Sundays : the lessons and legacy of James Arthur West
 (1895-1988) / by Ben Witherington, III.
Description: Macon, GA : Smyth & Helwys Publishing, 2022.
Identifiers: LCCN 2022051428 | ISBN 9781641734165 (paperback)
Subjects: LCSH: Christian education--Textbooks for adults--Baptists.
Classification: LCC BX6225 .W47 2022 | DDC 268/.861--dc23/eng/20230110
LC record available at https://lccn.loc.gov/2022051428

Disclaimer of Liability: With respect to statements of opinion or fact available in this work of nonfiction, Smyth & Helwys Publishing Inc. nor any of its employees, makes any warranty, express or implied, or assumes any legal liability or responsibility for the accuracy or completeness of any information disclosed, or represents that its use would not infringe privately-owned rights.

Advance Praise for *Twice on Sundays*

James Arthur West saved lives on a regular basis as a fire chief. Now in this collection of his lessons, we have a unique window into the soul of one who also shaped lives as a Sunday school teacher. His love for God is evident, and his teachings offer in a vivid way his love for the sacred word.

Ben Witherington III has gathered a meaningful collection of his "Pop's" best teachings. Lovingly curated by a gifted scholar, a year's worth of lessons await the reader in this volume. There are 110 in all, because in those days churches always met "twice on Sundays." Witherington has spiffed up here and there but mostly brings forward his grandfather's own words. Enjoy these seasoned gems of wisdom and faith.

For generations, dedicated Sunday school teachers have delivered lessons that influenced real lives. We have a rare gift here because the family of one such teacher, James Arthur West, preserved decades of his hand-written lessons. Now you can enjoy the very best of them, collected here by scholar and grandson Ben Witherington III.

—Charles Qualls
Senior pastor, Franklin Baptist Church
Franklin, Virginia

God bless the Sunday school teachers like Ben's grandfather! One of my father's greatest joys was the Sunday school class he taught. He taught the "Ambassadors," and if memory serves me right, he taught that class every Sunday for nearly four decades. He loved teaching. He also loved preparing his classes. I once crossed the living room about 4:30 a.m. (I was a paper boy) and caught my father on his knees praying. He was praying for his class. He loved to teach books of the Bible, and his favorite commentaries were those written by the Plymouth Brethren. Every page in *Twice on Sundays* reminds me of my father teaching. There's something about faithful Sunday school teachers that makes the church go round.

—Scot McKnight
Professor of New Testament
Northern Seminary

In this unique devotional guide, Ben Witherington recovers insightful Sunday school lessons his grandfather wrote, then reflects on and dialogues with them. I found myself drawn into timeless biblical truths through their conversations with biblical texts, each other, what it meant to take the Bible as a daily guide and inspiration two generations ago, and what it means today. Sometimes, spiritual maturity spans generations, and this volume puts the challenges, concerns, and cultural issues of our time in a fresh perspective.

—R. Alan Culpepper
Emeritus Dean and Professor of New Testament
McAfee School of Theology, Mercer University

As the son and grandson of Baptist pastors, and, like the author, a child of the Sixties, I found *Twice on Sundays* a comfortable and familiar place. Its challenges are still our challenges, and Witherington's reflections a reminder that the life of faith is truly a life well lived.

—(The Rev. Dr.) William Brosend
Emeritus Professor of New Testament and Preaching
School of Theology
The University of the South
Sewanee, Tennessee

The spiritual wisdom of laypersons is often overlooked in the life of the church. In this book, Ben Witherington shares the spiritual insights from Sunday school lessons taught by his grandfather, James Arthur West, a deacon and Sunday school teacher in a Baptist church in Wilmington, North Carolina. West's lessons are insightful and wise, grouped in fifty-two pairs of lessons, to which Witherington adds his own questions and thoughts for reflection. This book provides a rich devotional guide through biblical truth with spiritual wisdom for an individual or group.

—Dr. Steve Lemke
Provost Emeritus and Distinguished Professor of
Philosophy and Ethics
New Orleans Baptist Theological Seminary

TWICE ON SUNDAYS

THE LESSONS AND LEGACY OF JAMES ARTHUR WEST (1895–1988)

Selected, edited, and reflected on by his grandson,
BEN WITHERINGTON III

Also by Ben Witherington III

Encounters with Jesus

Voices and Views on Paul (with Jason A. Myers)

Who God Is: Meditations on the Character of Our God

Priscilla: The Life of an Early Christian

Biblical Theology: The Convergence of the Canon

Matthew (Smyth & Helwys Bible Commentary)

Torah Old and New: Exegesis, Intertextuality, and Hermeneutics

James Arthur West
1895–1988

Contents

Foreword by Dr. Todd D. Still	xi
Introduction: A Life Well Lived	1
Preface	5
First Sunday of the Year	9
Second Sunday of the Year	13
Third Sunday of the Year	17
Fourth Sunday of the Year	21
Fifth Sunday of the Year	25
Sixth Sunday of the Year	29
Seventh Sunday of the Year	33
Eighth Sunday of the Year	37
Ninth Sunday of the Year	41
Tenth Sunday of the Year	45
Eleventh Sunday of the Year	49
Twelfth Sunday of the Year	55
Thirteenth Sunday of the Year	59
Fourteenth Sunday of the Year	65
Fifteenth Sunday of the Year	71
Sixteenth Sunday of the Year	75
Seventeenth Sunday of the Year	79
Eighteenth Sunday of the Year	83
Nineteenth Sunday of the Year	87
Twentieth Sunday of the Year	91
Twenty-first Sunday of the Year	97
Twenty-second Sunday of the Year	103

Twenty-third Sunday of the Year	109
Twenty-fourth Sunday of the Year	113
Twenty-fifth Sunday of the Year	117
Twenty-sixth Sunday of the Year	121
Twenty-seventh Sunday of the Year	127
Twenty-eighth Sunday of the Year	131
Twenty-ninth Sunday of the Year	135
Thirtieth Sunday of the Year	141
Thirty-first Sunday of the Year	145
Thirty-second Sunday of the Year	149
Thirty-third Sunday of the Year	155
Thirty-fourth Sunday of the Year	161
Thirty-fifth Sunday of the Year	167
Thirty-sixth Sunday of the Year	171
Thirty-seventh Sunday of the Year	177
Thirty-eighth Sunday of the Year	183
Thirty-ninth Sunday of the Year	187
Fortieth Sunday of the Year	191
Forty-first Sunday of the Year	195
Forty-second Sunday of the Year	203
Forty-third Sunday of the Year	209
Forty-fourth Sunday of the Year	215
Forty-fifth Sunday of the Year	221
Forty-sixth Sunday of the Year	227
Forty-seventh Sunday of the Year	233
Forty-eighth Sunday of the Year	237
Forty-ninth Sunday of the Year	241
Fiftieth Sunday of the Year	245
Fifty-first Sunday of the Year	251
Fifty-second Sunday of the Year	257
Postscript	263

Foreword

Ben Witherington III is a close friend of mine. Come to think of it, I regard Ben to be something akin to an older brother. As a senior, seasoned scholar, he has certainly been an encourager and mentor to me. Over the years, we have shared many meals together, attended conferences together, worked on projects together (particularly the Lightfoot Legacy Project), taught at each other's schools, and been in one another's homes. Additionally, last year, Jason Myers and I co-edited a book of essays in Ben's honor (*Rhetoric, History, and Theology: Interpreting the New Testament* [Fortress Academic]). Presently, Ben and I are looking forward to leading a group of pilgrims to biblical sites in Greece and Turkey. Ben and I are friends, close friends.

Friends share things with one another. Occasionally, Ben and I will send one other writing samples for feedback. Not long after Ben's mother passed away, he began to share with me select lessons and devotionals from his maternal grandfather's ("Pop," as Ben called him) notebooks, which his mom had kept over the passing years. Having read the first selection Ben sent to me, I wrote to him, "This is beautiful, Ben, and I am so grateful that you shared it with me. I daresay the substance and insight demonstrated by your grandfather in this eloquently written excerpt outstrip not a few seminary-trained individuals today. His knowledge and love for the Lord and for Scripture are wonderfully expressed. What a remarkable heritage that is yours, to which you have contributed appreciably, indeed inestimably." Having received and read a number of other selections, I began to think to myself, "These are thoughtful and insightful, encouraging and life-giving. They should be and need to be shared with a broader audience."

When my Methodist friend, Ben, asked me, a Baptist, who might be willing and able to publish the best of his Baptist grandfather's preserved reflections on Scripture and the Christian life, I suggested Smyth & Helwys. I then, in turn, recommended "Pop's" words and work to my friend of years Keith Gammons. It delights me, therefore, to see this worthwhile project in print.

In *Twice on Sundays*, one will not only discover over ond hundred meaningful lessons and devotions from a devout Baptist layman, who lived long and well, but one will also find reflections upon and questions arising from these entries from one of the most prolific and respected evangelical biblical scholars of the late twentieth and early twenty-first centuries. Over time, Baptists have frequently described themselves as being "people of the book." If I am unsure whether that descriptor is (now) true in general, I am absolutely sure this was the case for James Arthur West, who was steeped in and shaped by sacred Scripture.

I am no less convinced that this volume, regardless of how it is read, will nourish the sympathetic, Christian reader. In fact, I suspect that readers of this book will be surprised time and again by the simple profundity and profound piety of this Baptist layman's biblical, theological, and personal reflections. When Nathaniel wondered if anything good could come out of Nazareth, he was told by Philip to "Come and see" (John 1:45-46). For those who may wonder if this volume is worth your time, energy, and money, here is what I would say to you—"Taste and see." Then, once you have done so, redouble your commitment to be a student, if not a teacher, of Scripture and a doer of the Word on every day that ends with "y."

—Todd D. Still
DeLancey Dean and Hinson Professor
Baylor University, Truett Seminary
Waco, Texas

Introduction

A Life Well Lived

It was a very hot summer night in Wilmington, North Carolina, somewhere between 1954 and 1960 when Pop was the fire chief of the fire department. Since I remember what happened and could describe the event, it must have been close to 1960 when I was eight. The fire bell had been installed upstairs in the hall in the West home at 1319 Princess Street. I was sleeping in the bedroom right next to where the bell was. It went off in the middle of the night and was loud enough to wake the dead. It scared the daylights out of me as a young boy. I heard Pop get up and throw on his fire gear, and run down the stairs to get into his red car with the light on top to go to another fire. There was no hope of my going back to sleep. For one thing there was no air conditioning in this house and I had been sweating and sticking to the sheets. So, I went downstairs and opened the front door hoping for a little breeze to come across the front porch. I sat on the bottom step of the stairs waiting for Pop's return.

Eventually, after dawn, here came my grandfather smelling of smoke, with his fire gear and chief's hat still on. He walked in and I said in a quiet voice, "So what happened, Pop?" He then described to me a harrowing scene at a burning apartment building, with him rushing in to save some folks. I remember him mentioning a small child. It led to my asking him a question, since this seemed such a dangerous enterprise and I knew he wasn't being paid a lot of money.

I said "Pop, why are you such a straight arrow? Why are you always working so hard to help other people?" His reply was succinct and memorable: "Hell is too hot, and heaven too sweet to mess around in this life. You gotta keep one eye on eternity." I will never forget that answer.

James Arthur West was not just a fireman and a fire chief, he was also a devout Christian, a deacon at Temple Baptist Church and a Sunday school teacher. I have exactly no memory of him being the latter, but as my sister and I have been going through our mother's effects, Laura found his spiral notebooks full of his Sunday school and devotional lessons. They are all written out in beautiful cursive script verbatim, all dated and usually with a Scriptural text cited. According to the dates on the surviving lessons, these were given in the 1960s through the end of the 1980s. I do not remember hearing one of these, or for that matter seeing him write them down, but then I would not have been in his adult Sunday school class when I was visiting as a child or young adult.

These lessons revealed to me a side and depth of my grandfather that I did not know existed before recently. He was a profound reader of the Bible, and he drew much wisdom from it for those whom he taught. In fact, I have been astounded by some of his reflections in these lessons and wish I had known all about this before he passed away. I remember him sending me religious articles between 1974 and 1977 when I was in seminary, but never his own writings, always a religious column from the Wilmington paper. In some ways I feel like the man in the New Testament who was rummaging around in the dirt and suddenly found the pearl of great price unexpectedly. And having read many of these lessons, I realized quickly Pop's pearls of wisdom deserve to be shared, and that is what follows in this book along with some commentary and my expansion and reflection on some of his seminal ideas. During the course of reading and transcribing all his Sunday school lessons, I found his own personal testimony, which I share at this juncture. The following are Pop's own words about a change in his life.

***

Many years ago, there was a young lady who had joined the church at twelve years of age and six years later she suddenly realized that nothing had happened in her life to make it meaningful for Christ. She felt as if there was something missing in her life and she didn't know quite what to do about it. She was a very fine Christian, she attended Sunday school and church and read her Bible regularly but she felt that this was not enough.

She became restless because of this frustration and then on a Sunday night at church the pastor said, "We are so happy that we have been able to fill all our teaching positions but one, but surely there is someone in the church to teach this class of eight-to-ten-year-old children. I beg of you to not allow this important place go unfulfilled. They must have a teacher, so will someone please volunteer." At this, that young lady held up her hand not quite realizing what she was doing or the consequences. She took the class and in a very short time she was in love with her work and those children and soon she was loved by the class. She told them about her past Christian life and how the class brought her joy. One by one the children in that class began to join the church.

This young lady was a wonderful person and a good teacher. One of the boys in her class went home one Sunday evening after church and asked his mother if he could join the church next Sunday. She said, "If you feel the same way next Sunday you may join the church." Then on Monday in the late afternoon the mother said, "Come with me," and they went to a bluff where they could see the Cape Fear River below, and over the tree tops beyond. It was just before sunset and there were small white clouds floating around with the sun peeping through and as the sun sank behind the trees, gold and red streaks of sunlight filtered through making a beautiful sight. The mother said "Son, God put those clouds and the rays of the sun there, that vegetation might grow so that we can live. God made the flowers and everything in the world."

The next Sunday the boy joined the church, and wanted a Bible all his own so he saved his pennies and found a testament he wanted and when he had saved enough he bought it and was one happy boy. For many years he carried that testament with him and read it in his spare time wherever he was. Today, I still have that testament and I wouldn't part with it. A good Sunday school program should be and was the foundation of my church. Isn't what the young lady did, what Christ is asking us to do, carry on his mission to a lost world?

This testimony is about something that happened to my grandfather somewhere in the period 1903 to 1905, for he was ten in 1905. And clearly it bore much fruit, for these Sunday school lessons he wrote are from sixty to eighty years later!! It is a blessing to share them now.

***

Since the Baptists used to have church both morning and evening on Sundays, I have set this book up to present two sets of fifty-two lessons for each of the Sundays in the year. There are many more lessons, but I've selected the ones that seemed most telling and helpful. They are brief, and I've added reflection questions as well as some of my own thoughts after each one. I've also arranged these lessons or devotions according to the church calendar to some degree. I should add that while I agree with about 98 percent of what my grandfather said in these devotions, occasionally I didn't agree with his interpretation, but I let him have his say, and only once in a while made a corrective editorial comment where needed. The important thing was to allow his Christian wisdom to come through loud and clear. Occasionally, when a lesson seemed incomplete, I added a sentence or two in the same vein in the lesson itself.

In an age when even the church is becoming more and more biblically illiterate, these lessons are a timely reminder of how important it is to be well grounded in the Word and in one's relationship with the Lord when the cultural winds blowing in other directions are so strong, and the world is in the chaos of pandemics and wars. From my vantage point, this food for the soul came unexpectedly like manna from heaven.

Finally, if you are curious as to where the phrase twice on Sundays comes from, it was first found in print before the Revolutionary War as follows: "Preaching once every Day (twice on Sundays)" was printed in the *South-Carolina Gazette* (Charleston, SC) on December 8, 1746. Sundays should be a time to worship and fellowship with fellow Christians and to reflect on the meaning of Christian life. It should be a time to spend more time in God's Word, perhaps catch up on one's devotions and Christian lessons. I can think of few resources that can better help you in that endeavor than these lessons from James Arthur West, my grandfather. I hope they will nourish those consuming these reflections.

—Ben Witherington III
July 15, 2022

Preface

The following two lessons deserve to be read first, to give a clear picture of how my grandfather viewed the Bible, as God's Word in the words of human beings. What follows thereafter makes better sense having reflected on the credo that these two lessons reflect.

Facts about the Bible
9/29/74 and 8/3/75

The Bible was the first printed book and is the best-selling book in the world. 8,000,000 are printed in the United States each year, and 35 million throughout the world. If you counted five to a family, it would mean 7 million families are without Bibles. Parts of the Bible have been printed in over 1,100 languages and dialects. The first complete English translation was printed in 1384. The first American edition was printed in an Indian language at Cambridge, Massachusetts, in 1661. The second Bible was printed in Pennsylvania in 1743.

The Bible is composed of 66 books and written by about 36 authors in a period of about 1,600 years. The King James or Authorized Version was first printed in 1611. The purpose set forth in the Old Testament unfolded the redemption plan of God for the human race and therefore had its fulfillment in the birth, life, ministry, miraculous works, death resurrection, and exaltation of Jesus Christ. The New Testament is the authentic and divinely inspired record of these notable events and the teachings of the Messiah, and it unfolds to the world the doctrines of Christianity.

This book called the Bible contains the mind of God, the state of humankind, the way of salvation, the doom of sinners, and the happiness of believers. Its doctrines are holy, its precepts are binding, its histories are true, and its decisions are immutable. Read it to be wise, believe it to be safe, and practice it to be holy. It contains light to direct you, food to support you and comfort to cheer you. It is the traveler's map, the pilgrim's staff, the pilot's compass, the soldier's sword and the Christian's charter. Here paradise is restored, heaven opened, and the gates of Hell disclosed. Christ is its grand subject, our good its design, and the glory of God its end. It should fill the memory, rule the heart, and guide the feet. Read it slowly, frequently, prayerfully. It is a mine of wealth, a paradise of glory, and a river of pleasure. It is given to you in this life, will be opened at the judgment, and be remembered forever. It involves the highest responsibility, rewards the greatest labor, and condemns all those who trifle with its holy contents. This friend will all our needs supply. This fountain sends forth streams of joy. This good Physician gives us health. This sun renews and warms the soul. This sword both wounds and heals and makes us whole. This book shows us our sins forgiven. This guide conducts us safely to heaven. This charter has been sealed with blood. This volume is the Word of God. FOLLOW IT.

Then, on 8/3/75 Pop said this about the Bible:

The new Christian first needs to establish his faith in the Bible for it is the Word of God. The Bible is not a book of philosophy, although it is philosophical. Don't expect the Bible to be a scientific treatise. However, there is no discrepancy between ascertained facts of science and the Bible. The Bible is not a book of history but is found to be accurate when it records history. The Bible was given to humankind from God, revealing Jesus Christ the Son of God and God the Son, the only Savior. He is the center and the circumference. It is Christ from Genesis to Revelation. The Bible is as high above other books as the heavens are above the earth. Someone has said of the Bible—read it to be wise, believe it to be safe, and practice it to be right.

To an interested student of the Bible, it inspires him to search continually for more truths. The Bible is also a difficult book because if humans entirely understood it, it would be a natural book, but in fact it is a spiritual book, and yet it is designed to govern the thoughts, words, and actions of human beings. There is no other book that can compare with it. It commands the believer to study the Scriptures.

God says, "Ask and you shall receive, seek and you shall find, knock and the door shall be opened to you." So you see the Bible, in one sense, is a book of positive thinking. It opens our minds and inspires us to ask God's help, to seek His answers, and to knock at His door that we might receive His blessings and be eligible to hear the welcoming words "Well done, good and faithful servant; enter into the joy of the Lord." The Bible does not always give us the answers we might like, but it does provide us with a solution to our problems if we will but listen to that still, small voice found throughout the Bible.

First Sunday of the Year

The Existence of God
8/10/75

The Bible reveals God as the only Infinite and Eternal Being, having no beginning and no ending. He is creator and sustainer of all things. He is the supreme Personal Intelligence and Righteous Ruler of His universe. He is Life, and therefore the only source of life. Human beings are natural and cannot truly know God by human wisdom. The Bible says, "Can you by searching find out God?" God is a person, and can be truly known only by revelation. In the Old Testament He revealed Himself to and through the Prophets. In the New Testament He reveals Himself through Jesus Christ. The Bible nowhere attempts to prove or argue for the existence of God. The existence of the true God is taken to be a fact. In the beginning God . . . . The Bible begins by announcing the sublime fact of God and His existence. Universal belief in God comes from within human beings, created in His image.

Everything that ever began owes its existence to a cause. We have a watch, there must be a watchmaker. We have a building, there must be a builder. We have a creation, there must be a creator. This creation could not have come into existence without an intelligent, personal Creator any more than the alphabet could produce a book itself without an author. The Bible and the Christ it reveals, His virginal conception, His sinless life, His vicarious death, and His bodily resurrection, all this and much more argue for the existence of God. The Bible reveals God as a personality. He is called the living and true God, one possessing self-consciousness and self-determination. His personality is shown in what He does. He loves ("he so loved the world"). He hates, in Proverbs 6.16 we find six things the Lord hates.

He cares ("he cares for you," 1 Pet 5.7). He grieves ("it grieved his heart," Gen 6.6). Only a person, a personality can love, hate, care, and grieve. Therefore, God must be a living, eternal, personal being.

There are four definitions in the Bible. Since God cannot be fully defined, they are incomplete, but throw light upon the nature of God. God is love—this is His very nature, he has divine compassion for human beings. God is light. This too is His nature in His divine character. In Him is no darkness at all. God is consuming fire. This is the nature of His divine holiness. God is spirit, this is His nature in His divine essence. The attributes of God reveal His nature.

Life is ascribed to God. All knowledge is ascribed to God. All power is ascribed to God. Filling the universe with His presence is ascribed to God. God is everywhere present, but He is not in everything. If God were in everything, human beings could worship any object and they would be worshiping God. God is spirit, and those that worship Him must worship Him in spirit and truth. Grace is the love and mercy of God in action. His grace is both sufficient and it does not discriminate. His grace justifies and makes every believer an heir with Christ.

God's Plan Fulfilled
11/9/75

The Son of God was present at the meeting of the Trinity when that voice broke the silence of eternity announcing that human beings would be made in the image of God. He was there when God breathed in through the nostrils the breath of life and man became a living being. God made human beings, so He knows them. But has this modern world some new insight, something that outstripped even Jesus in wisdom about the salvation of the world? Is there a streamlined method of saving the world? NO!

God's plan is the only plan for salvation of the world. People for two thousand years have tried to find shortcuts to salvation but to no avail. The plan that Jesus brought to earth, to seek and save that which is lost is the only plan. Every Christian is a living letter for Christ to a troubled world. Your life and my life, if we are Christians is a living letter for the Kingdom of Christ. If it is not, then we are remiss in our lives as Christians.

Jesus was not unmindful of the difficulties involved in carrying the Gospel to a lost world. He was wounded for our sins. He had to agonize in Gethsemane, stand firm before Pilate, and carry His cross up the hill of Calvary and die an unthinkable death for us. Every human being is dear to Christ, everyone counts to Him, a poor man has a chance, a sick man can get well, an ignorant man can become wise, a good man can become better, and a dead man can be made alive in Jesus Christ. Christ has paid the supreme price for us. The apostles understood this glorious Gospel to be for the wide world. We are not to preach tolerance and philanthropy, but rather Christ crucified. It is our duty to establish relationships between human beings, between races, between nations, by means of the Gospel. The Gospel is Good News that whosoever believes in Him shall not perish but have everlasting life. I am glad there is no puzzle to put together, no mystery to solve—just believe in Him. This Gospel is the world's greatest love story, and it is what we need to hear, and to be happy that it has been our privilege to know this love.

Questions and Thoughts for Reflection

1. Have you noticed that there is no organization that adamantly opposes the existence of unicorns even though no one has seen one in the wild, or a club that argues that gravity doesn't exist, even though no one can see it? And yet there are organizations promoting the notion that there is no God. Why? Why are these people trying so hard to banish God from the public sphere and our lives in general *if God doesn't even exist?* The answer is not hard to find. Deep down these persons, created in God's image, know there is a God (see Rom 1.18-32), but they want to exorcise His presence from their minds, their hearts their very lives. But it's a losing battle. It's like Sisyphus endlessly pushing that rock up the hill and never reaching the top. The psalmist sums up the dilemma—"the fool says in his heart 'there is no God.'" If you know people like this, you should pray for them, for they have hardened their hearts. Arguing with them will not likely change their views. Loving them and praying for them,

and being there for them when they need you, may change their lives. Ask yourself—Have I made any effort to help a person who is adamantly atheistic?

2. In this lesson, my grandfather reminds us that "we are not to preach tolerance and philanthropy but rather 'Christ crucified.'" What do you think he meant by this? In our day and age, the term tolerance has come to mean acceptance even of all kinds of lifestyles that the Bible says are immoral. But tolerance is not the same thing as acceptance and agreement. When a culture starts redefining the meaning of terms like tolerance or even husband and wife, you know our culture is in trouble. My grandfather suggests that the preaching of Christ and Him crucified is the first step back away from the precipice of national disaster. Do you agree? Why or why not?

Second Sunday of the Year

1/9/77

"For we know that all things work together for good for those that love God." —Romans 8.28

This year is a new year, today is a new day, this minute is a new minute, time marches on. Last year is gone forever, all things are new. I believe in the beauty, the possibilities and the promises of this new year. Seeds that are now sleeping in the bosom of the earth will awaken, break through the surface of the soil, and become sturdy plants, fragrant flowers, and some of them, nourishing food. Trees that are now barren of leaves will burst forth in the Spring to provide assurance, shade, and fruit as they have since time began. Tiny babies will develop into healthy children who will be loved, cared for, and nurtured. Ugly caterpillars will become beautiful butterflies. Dreams will become realities, God's sun will rise each morning, His rain will fall, His mountains will stand, and His rainbows will give radiant promise of ever greater tomorrows.

Ideas that now lie dormant in the minds of persons will find complete expression this year. Poems and books that are now unknown will mature into classics of wisdom and inspiration. Our prayers will be heard and answered. Friendships will be formed and strengthened. Difficulties will be met and mastered. Challenges will be faced and conquered. Victories will be achieved and celebrated. I confidently expect this to be a great year in our history, a year when God's truth will be realized, His love expressed, His joy experienced, and His presence felt by people who never knew Him before. I believe this because the Scripture says, "God works all things together for good for those who love Him." Not everything in itself is or will be good, but God can work all things together for good.

This new year is an opportunity for each of us to fix our thoughts on what is true and right, because we have been born anew to a living hope through the resurrection of Jesus Christ from the dead. God is a God of hope that lights our pathway brighter for each tomorrow. Jesus said "Behold I make all things new" for a reason.

8/10/69

"What is a human being that thou art mindful of him?" —Psalm 8.4

In the beginning God created the heaven and the earth. He didn't use the words heaven and earth in the plural sense but in the singular. Nevertheless, human beings are determined to find life on the other creations of God. God made all things and all creatures, and the last of His handiwork was man and woman, and after He had made them He said it was good, in fact very good. And He gave them dominion over the material world. And yes, He loves human beings above all else.

But the militarist says, "Humans aren't much, just an instrument to stand by the cannon and the gun, the battleship and the sub awaiting orders and willing to take the consequences." The dictator says, "Humans are not much, just the means by which my wishes are fulfilled, the chief concern is the strength of the state, not the happiness of the individual." The materialist and the atheist say, "Humans aren't much. The multitudes of suns, stars, the duration of time, the magnitude of the universe make of human beings nothing but specks of dust. Their lives are short and their values die with them."

But God, who knew what was in human beings, created in His image, begged to differ, and gave His life for us. He looks on us very differently. For Jesus, human beings are unique creations of God. A human being's worth is not limited to the weight of his body. His worth is seen in his relationship to his family, his neighbors, his state, his church, his God. A fine exercise is to examine ourselves in the light of these relationships. However poor we may be, whatever our birth, whatever may be our lot, some value may be found in our lives and this worth is acknowledged when God gave His only Son to rescue us. If today finds you discouraged and life seems empty, remember there is One who came into our midst, knew us to our very core and came that we might be redeemed, and beyond that have life abundantly.

Questions and Thoughts for Reflection

1. In the first lesson for this Sunday, Pop reflects on the providence of God, His ability to work all things together for good. But notice the Scripture does not say He does this for everyone, rather it specifies that He does it for those who love Him and are called according to purpose or choice, as the Greek says. Implicit in this verse, and clearly affirmed in various places in my grandfather's lessons is that God is the source of all that is gracious and good, but He is absolutely not the source of things that are wicked or evil. In other words, God is not the only actor in the universe, there are also angelic and human beings who have wills and can make choices, choices that they make according to their own inclinations and reasonings, not because they were destined to do so. Most of the evil we encounter in the world is caused by sinful human beings.

Natural disasters are not inherently evil. They are merely examples of human beings getting in the way of nature. For example, if there is a major earthquake or fire on a desert island in the middle of an ocean, no one takes notice, and it is not even considered a disaster. It is simply a natural process. Notice as well that 1 Kings 19 suggests that you cannot read the will of God by analyzing natural disasters—"but the Lord was not in the fire, not in the earthquake" despite insurance companies calling such things acts of God. As that same text suggests, to know God's will you have to listen to His Word and seek His guidance. How would you evaluate Romans 8.28 and apply it in your everyday life?

2. The second lesson for today involves seeing human beings as created in God's image, and seeing them as God sees them. This is important because we often hear pronouncements from people ranging from philosophers to politicians that take a very cynical

view of human nature on the one hand, or alternatively a very naïve view that human beings are basically good. Neither is the appropriate perspective. The Bible teaches human beings are all of sacred worth, but they are also all fallen creatures with sinful inclinations. The image of God in them has not been destroyed such that they are unredeemable, but it has been badly distorted and damaged by sin and sinful inclinations, the chief of which is 'the heart turned in upon itself' namely our inherent self-centeredness, our inherent narcissism. What do you think my grandfather meant when he said you can tell a lot about a person and his character by how he relates to God, his neighbors, his family, his church? What other telltale signs of a person can you list?

Third Sunday of the Year

The Relevance of the Gospel
7/20/75

We venture into the conflict in our lives everyday not in fear but in faith that Christ and His Word will be vindicated as we pursue the light He gives to us. We are always sensitive to that which is around us and we are really concerned with our brothers and sisters. We are not building walls around us to insulate ourselves so we won't know what is happening, but we remain responsive, involved and obedient to God. We do not have a personal Gospel and a social Gospel. There is but one Gospel and one Gospel only and that is the Gospel of God. This indivisible message from God has its individual and its social application. It has the power to redeem the social order. In the world where we live, nothing can be finally irrelevant. *Therefore, it is impossible to argue about religious faith on the basis of relevance. We must instead insist on the irrelevance of relevance and argue on the basis of truth and truth's claims.* The solutions to the problems of existence are to be found in God, the living personal God. The first word of Christianity is GOD. Christianity founds its whole system of truths, its view of the universe upon the existence of God.

To commit something to God requires honesty. There can be no thought of calculated risks, no maneuvering for advantage, no bargaining with God, no conditions set, no strings attached, no ifs, ands, or buts. Just commitment into the Lord's hands. This means total transfer. No predetermined outcomes are anticipated. Nothing is hidden or covered. David prayed in such honesty and such earnestness when he said, "Search me O God and know my heart. Try me and know my thoughts and see if there be any wicked way in me, and lead me in the way everlasting." This speaks of an honesty that leaves everything transparent in God's sight—every motive, every thought, every deed is presented to God and committed into His hands. Commitment means to place our lives in the beam of God's searchlight so that we walk in the light as He is in the light. Such honesty with God, with others, with ourselves allows God to do what He desires in our lives without our interference, bringing to pass His will. Blessed is the person who does this.

10/18/70

". . . whosoever hears these sayings of mine, and does them, I will liken him to a wise man who built his house upon a rock."
—Matthew 7.24

Our forefathers founded this nation on the rock of God's Word. Today people buy more Bibles and know less about the Bible's teaching than ever before. The result is a spiritual depression more serious than the economic one. By neglecting the religious principles once reverenced, our nation has slipped from the rock to shifting sand. Daniel Webster left this warning: "If we abide by the principle taught in the Bible our country will go on prospering. . . . But if we and our posterity neglect its instructions and authority no one can tell how sudden a catastrophe may overwhelm us and bury our glory in profound obscurity."

The only way back to real stability is by restoring the Bible to its rightful place in our homes, and Christ in our hearts, and love for our fellow human beings. If prosperity should return under our present low moral standards it would mean more drinking, more deaths on the highways, more gambling, more divorces and suicides, and more gun violence.

First, we must have a moral and spiritual recovery, for "except the Lord build the house, they labor in vain who build it." Our citizens must turn again to the Bible, to the church, and to God. We must undergird our character with the Biblical truths and teach our children from the Word of God, gather every Lord's Day in God's house to study the ways of life, then say with Joshua, "as for me and my house, we will serve the Lord." When we become a Bible-revering people once again, our nation shall stand on a rock where no storms can shake it. Is your house built upon that rock?

Questions and Thoughts for Reflection

1. What do you think Pop meant by the irrelevance of relevance when decisions must be made on the basis of God's existence and truth? We speak a lot these days about transparency, wanting the police, politicians, other authority figures to be honest and transparent. But what about our own need to be transparent with God? While it may seem odd, some people who believe in God aren't really all that transparent when they pray to God. Do they really think you can hide something from an all-knowing God? Why are there so many exhortations in the Bible to confess our sins? Surely part of the answer is so that we will not be self-deceived about our lives nor dishonest in the way we relate to God. So much of our modern conversation is about what is "relevant," and because of this concept many, many thoughts, ideas, concepts from the past are dismissed out of hand as not germane to what we are dealing with now. What are the problems that can arise when we fail or deliberately dismiss the lessons from the past which can indeed be helpful and pertinent to our current dilemmas?

2. It is a common assertion by conservative Christians who both love God and love America, that our country was founded by devout Christians and our foundational documents such as the Declaration of Independence, the Constitution, and the Bill of Rights reflect profound Christian values we need to recover if there is to be revival in our country. In fact, all of this is at best a half-truth. There *were* some very devout Christians who helped found our country, such as Samuel Adams or perhaps George Washington and some of the Quakers such as William Penn, but there were also some Deists who did not like the miraculous aspects in the Bible. This included most crucially Thomas Jefferson (who along with Adams and Franklin were the chief drafters of the Declaration) who also produced a truncated version of the New Testament with the miraculous material expunged, and to a lesser degree John Adams, and certainly included Benjamin Franklin, never mind folks like Thomas Paine.

What the Founding Fathers were concerned about, when it came to religion, is that there would not be an official governmentally sponsored religion—which in their day meant they didn't want the America government to be politically aligned with any particular Catholic or Protestant denomination. Freedom of religious affiliation was what was affirmed. This did not mean in the eighteenth century "the separation of church and state" in the modern sense of that phrase. It meant actually the opposite of what it has come to mean now—namely the Founding Fathers wanted to protect the church from the state's interference and dictates. They were not interested in protecting the state from various Christian principles and ethics, which are indeed to some degree encoded in our founding documents. In view of this history, and where we are today, what would a revival look like in our country, and what general religious principles and ethics, such as issues of justice and economic opportunity could be affirmed in such a revival? Would a recovery of a wide belief in the sanctity of unborn as well as born life be a part of such a revival?

Fourth Sunday of the Year

5/16/71

"And the vessel that he made of clay was marred in the hand of the potter. So, he made it again, another vessel as seemed good to the potter to make it." —Jeremiah 18.4

Before Jeremiah received instruction from God to visit the potter, because of his ministry in Judah, and because of the heavy burden he felt, he went around tearing down things, destroying and overthrowing what he came in contact with. God had given him charge over the nations with instructions to tear down, but also to build and to plant that the nation might be redeemed. But Jeremiah had not fully understood God's instructions so it became necessary for God to do something to make Jeremiah understand more fully what His plan was for the Judaean nation. Thus, God caused Jeremiah to visit the potter and to fully observe the potter at work, doing this visit while the potter was working. The vessel he made involved his making a slightly wrong move, and in just a second the vessel was completely destroyed, and the potter was left with just a wad of clay, not a vessel. So, the potter had to start over again, and this time he completely finished a beautiful vessel.

I think I can understand what came into Jeremiah's mind when he began to see the greater purpose of God for the nation of Judah and for His work with this nation, so instead of tearing down he started building and planting that the nation might be redeemed.

On the outskirts of Los Angeles. I once visited a large pottery plant and saw many men at work making various pottery items and I saw what a glazed finish product would be like, and just what a mistake would do. In just a second a beautiful piece of pottery would be nothing but raw materials. Reading Jeremiah, I realized that God was able to take the most flawed, or even vile and mean human beings and make godly leaders of them. And I am sure Jeremiah realized this and applied it to his ministry.

9/6/70

"And Simon Peter stood and warmed himself. They said therefore unto him, are you not also one of his disciples? He denied it, saying 'I am not.'" —John 18.25

The Lord was on trial for His life. He was standing before the Jewish authorities, and then later the Roman governor who asked Him about truth, with a sneer. Impudent soldiers were mocking Him , ruffians were smiting Him . But where was Peter who only a short time ago had sworn such undying allegiance and had shown such bravery in protecting Jesus from the mob with his sword?

The night was cold, and Peter's blood was freezing because his heart was colder still. He was afraid of the consequences of being identified with Jesus. The soldiers and servants jostled each other to get near the blazing fire. So, Peter crowded in too. And all the while his Lord was on trial for His life. One can scarcely credit the fact that Simon Peter, of all people, was the one who should have shown such heartlessness, indifference, and infidelity. To think that Peter could have turned his back upon the sad scene at such a moment and stretched his shivering limbs before a soothing fire. Just what kind of man was he? Where was his loyalty? Where was his manhood?

In such a case, where would we stand? What would we do? Do we have the bravery or loyalty to put ourselves in jeopardy, or would we do as Peter did and deny that we knew Him? But let's not be too hard on Peter, until we are sure we would have acted differently had we been in his place. Then we should not be too easy on ourselves, for it is not too much to expect of us for whom Christ died that we should forget our own discomforts, and think of the Savior and His suffering, and mold our lives as one who owes all that He has to the Lamb who died on Calvary, for His love was so great for us all.

Questions and Thoughts for Reflection

1. If you evaluate the great Christian leaders of the last 2,000 or so years, there are many surprises along the way. Some of the world's worst scoundrels have been converted to Christian faith and become Christian leaders! And most basically the Christian Gospel, with its affirmation of the concept of conversion affirms that people can actually change. Indeed, if we didn't believe that, very few people would dedicate their lives to evangelism or missionary work. Redemption involves a person's life orientation and moral character changing because "all have sinned and fallen short of the glory of God." Among other things, this means that Christians should not write off anyone as unredeemable. Nor should they rule out a person from service in the Christian ministry simply because they have a dubious or even notorious past. There are today many good ministers who previously served time in prison, and were actually converted there. Do you believe God can take a broken vessel and make a new serviceable one out of it? This lesson from Jeremiah raises that very question.

2. In a sense, the second lesson for today about Peter's dramatic denial of Christ, presumably out of fear and an attempt at self-preservation, raises the opposite issue. What happens when a redeemed person acts out of Christian character, because obviously, Christians do sin? Notice that in James 5.16 James is exhorting Christians to come clean, to confess their sins to one another, and commit themselves to transparency. While Peter's dramatic denial is surprising, the beautiful story of his restoration in John 21 shows that God doesn't give up on us. Have you had incidents in your life where you acted against your Christian character? Did you repent and confess this to someone so you could be held accountable and not do it again? Have you had times in your life where you were under pressure and felt you had to lie? How did you respond in those situations?

Fifth Sunday of the Year

8/5/79

In today's world things are changing so fast that our understanding of religious truths must be constantly revised to keep pace with changing times and conditions. Just as there existed, traditionally, the seven deadly sins, so there are seven modern versions of these ancient errors. Today, the first deadly sin is ignorance. Ignorance is a sin because it blocks the free flow of the creative goodness of God. We need to know how evolution works, we need to understand population problems, ecology, our own aggressions, problems of community life, shortages of energy. Ignorance in these areas will frustrate the work of God because God doesn't change, we do. Arrogance is always a sin, and it comes from ignorance. *Being sure of yourself prevents your learning from others.* God meanwhile, is constantly revealing Himself anew.

Greed is a modern sin and is destructive to ourselves as well as others. Violence, like greed, is a modern sin and coercion destroys our freedom. Dishonesty is a modern sin. If God is love, then any word or act that misleads must be contrary to the will and goodness of God, and basic relationships are thereby damaged. Indifference is a modern sin as well. It is commonly assumed today that those in government can't be trusted. This applies in many areas of life, and even religious leaders and their religion have become suspect. The opposite of love is not hate, but rather indifference. The most tragic thing of all in the long run is the attitude that things don't matter, and despair rules the day. Our world is under great pressure, and when we get through hating, we turn away in indifference. The only way to solve our problems is to care more and more each day that we live.

The first of the original commandments is that we must love God with all our being with no substitution. Idolatry persists today and is equally dangerous as it was in Biblical times. We exalt ourselves or our achievements above those of the divine, making these things more important than God. Surely God is more than anything, any quality, any value, any idea or any achievement of human beings. God may reveal Himself in many ways, but the simple truth is if we accept God wholly and fully we will not be guilty of any of these seven deadly sins of the modern world—ignorance, arrogance, greed, violence, dishonesty, indifference, and idolatry. If we would rather go on growing in wisdom and understanding and in the depth and quality of our relationships with God and others, then these seven things must be rejected, shunned, condemned. As the Bible says, "Be sure your sins will find you out."

9/21/80

"To everything there is a season, and a time to every purpose under heaven." —Ecclesiastes 3.1

To all things worldly there is a beginning and a time to end, and then a new beginning is offered. In every age and culture human beings have felt the awesome presence of time. Our consciousness has been seared with the knowledge that all things worldly have a beginning and an end. Our lives are bracketed by the twin moments of birth and death. Our days dawn and set. We have come to know that time, its passage, its relentless motion is representative of the constancy and reliability of a great universal law. We cannot know our fate from one moment to the next. But we know with a certainty that the great wheel of beginning and end will turn and more importantly will repeat itself. Humanity has always honored those seasonal portals which passes in and out of the house of life. Humanity has always celebrated the arrival of Spring when new growth comes from a barren earth, when the sun once more invokes its blessings of light and warmth, when the creatures of the field awaken from their winter's sleep, when all nature seems to revive with a new vitality. At this most sacred moment, all humanity rejoices and pays tribute to the fulfillment of God's promise that a new cycle of time and life shall begin again.

Two thousand years ago during this same observance a great teacher and reformer sat with His disciples. His doctrine of love was to sweep across the face of half our globe, yet in a few brief hours He would be betrayed by one of His own, arrested, and put to the cross, and only then gathered into the glory of His Father on Easter Sunday. Human beings had brought the darkness of sin upon themselves, but through God's will humans will refute the darkness and bring new light and beauty to those around them with the Gospel.

And if we pray, let our prayers first implore our God never to silence the voice of conscience within us that we will be guided by its dictates. Then let our prayers be of thanks to God who in His wisdom has decreed that in due time, in the midst of the darkest of nights, through our own labors we shall pick up the candle and rekindle the light of understanding and love and the presage of a new and most glorious day when we will be with our Maker forever. Then we should thank God for the part He let us play in the endless pageant of life.

Questions and Thoughts for Reflection

1. My grandfather lists seven modern deadly sins. What do you think of the list? Is there anything you would add or leave out? Is ignorance really a sin? Perhaps he means willful ignorance. In any case, arrogance and ignorance are a very bad combination. What would you say are the major idolatries of America? I would add racism and various similar sorts of sin-based prejudices as one of the besetting sins of America. I would also add sexism, discrimination on the basis of sex. Even if only in the workplace, there should be equal pay for equal work whether done by women or men.

2. The New Testament does not say a lot about conscience, but it is important in Paul's writings. Unlike the modern notion of conscience the basic meaning of the word *suneidesis* is consciousness, and then as a derivative of that moral awareness. It doesn't simply refer to the little voice in your head that tells you no, or says "that would be a

bad idea." Conscience is indeed important because there isn't a rule for every occasion in the Bible.

For example, whether to buy this or that vehicle, and on what basis (this one is a gas guzzler but has more power, that one is a hybrid and saves both on fuel and on pollution but is a bit more expensive) is a decision about which one has to rely on conscience to help one decide what to do. This second lesson also raises the question about the seasons in life. I remember my orchestra teacher finally getting fed up with students watching the clock and so he put up a sign over it saying "time will pass, will you?" In one sense this is precisely what this lesson asks us to reflect on, not merely appreciating the endless changes in life, but understanding that God has decreed that there will be a goal, a finish line to time as we know it, and the question is—When we get there will we pass the test at the bema seat judgment of Christ?

Sixth Sunday of the Year

8/4/74

"Blessed are the peacemakers." —Matthew 5.9

There is much being said today about peace, world peace. Our President has been working toward that goal. But the truth of the matter is, we shall never have peace until we have peace with God. Every step we take toward God, we will be one step closer to peace.

I was asked the question that if I had a problem to come up should I quickly make a decision on it or should I take time to think about it first. I said think about it first. My friend said no, just give it time and maybe it will go away. But the truth is we will eventually have to face problems. Too many think if you just disregard a problem it will go away. How tragic this is to think you can pass up a problem and it will vanish. But in my search through my lesson collection I could not find a real answer to peace. So, then I turned to my Bible and Bible literature and started searching for an answer to this question and as I looked through the Bible I found "blessed are the peacemakers for they shall be called the children of God."

There are no simple answers to the pursuance of peace, but world peace should surely be our goal. Thus, we must begin with particulars rather than a general plan of action. God promises that for every step we take towards Him, that is a step for peace. Peacemaking is a noble vocation. But we cannot make peace with our own strength, any more than a brick mason can make a wall without a trowel, or a carpenter build a house without a hammer or an artist paint a picture without a brush.

To make peace on earth, we must know the peace of heaven. We must have the right equipment to do the job, and know the source of peace. There are 114 separate verses in the Bible that include the word peace. World peace cannot be found at the bargaining table. God is the one and only source of peace. In Leviticus we read that if we walk in God's will and in God's way we will have peace. Job says agree with God and you will have peace. The Psalmist says for you alone O God, make me dwell in peace. The angels said 'peace on earth among men with whom he is well pleased'. A man asked what has God to do with peace. If we are the least bit familiar with any sort of God-centered religion, we know that God gives peace in the heart, peace of mind and a personal peace and is also able to give world peace. As I studied and read, the same answer kept popping up in my mind. The cost of peace is personal righteousness. Yes, world peace can be achieved and it will come from the Prince of Peace.

World peace for the Christian will come with the return of the One who promised us an everlasting peace, a peace that passes all understanding. Jesus said when He was with us, "in me you may have peace." I believe therefore that we must pursue peace, pray for peace, live in peace, and we must be peacemakers. You ask what God has to do with peace? He is the source of peace and the price is our righteousness.

7/25/71

"There is no fear of God in their eyes." —Romans 3.18

Today, statistics show that the average individual has no fear of God. He or she does not live with eternity in view. He has forgotten that he is not an animal but rather is created in the image of God, a living soul. He is unaware that he will have to answer to God. *He who has no vision of eternity has no hold on time.*

I personally have had a long life to look back upon, and an eternity to look forward to. You don't hear much about eternity today. Perhaps this picture of humanity, with no fear of God in their eyes is morbid and dark but it is what the Bible says. The truth is that God looks on all who are outside of Christ, as lost, as part of the death sentence generation. But using what we are as a dark background he paints a radiant picture of what we can be in Jesus Christ. He says,

"If anyone is in Christ, he is new creature, old things are passed away, behold all things are become new." Through Christ we can experience a resurrection. He said, "I am come that you might have life and have it more abundantly." He also said, "I am the resurrection and the life. Whoever believes in me, though he were dead, yet shall he live."

Just as certainly as Jesus walked into the tomb of the dead Lazarus and called him forth alive, so also, He will impart to you His redeeming power, His life-giving resurrection power. He will change your nature so that instead of going out of the way, you will walk in His way. Instead of profanity and obscenity flowing from your mouth, it will be a well of praise and adoration to Him . He will take away your heart of stone and give you a new heart so that your every desire will be to please Him and serve your fellow human beings. And He will share your burdens, strengthen you and be a true companion who will guide your feet in life's perilous journey if you will only receive Him into your heart.

Questions and Thoughts for Reflection

1. Jesus blessed the peacemakers, not merely those who pursued personal peace in their own hearts. And yes, He is talking about peace between human beings. The reason they are blessed is because they are pursuing the same agenda as Jesus: "my peace I leave with you." But Jesus is talking about "shalom" not merely the absence of hostile activities, though that is involved (beating swords into plowshares says the prophet), but the presence of God which brings wholeness and healing—real shalom. Peace in one's own heart is easier to come by than peace between people, which is no doubt why a part of the great commandment is love your neighbor as yourself. We have to *pursue* it and work at it, in love. What do you think that the Bible means when it talks about the peace that passes human understanding? Do you agree with the notion that we will not have world peace until the Prince of Peace returns?

2. "He who has no vision of eternity, has no hold on time." What do you think my grandfather meant by that profound statement? To

me it seems to mean that we need to view all our days in the light of eternity as the goal of life. That in turn means we must do what the apostle exhorts us to do namely redeem the time, making the most of it, not wasting time. My grandfather was not a stern person at all, but he could not abide a frivolous wasting of good time or money or life. He was a man on a mission and time and life were there to be properly used. How do you evaluate your own use of time? Obviously, there is a time to work and a time to rest in each day, but what about the whole notion of retirement?

As a friend once said to me, "Retirement is not in the Bible, regular rest is." Should we be striving towards "leisure living" at the end of our days? How should a Christian assess such a notion? One thing is clear. Retirement as an idea and a life goal is something that came in modernity because of the industrial revolution and how worn-out workers became who did demanding manual labor of some kind. I used to laugh at the question Francis Asbury asked of his Methodist itinerant preachers at annual conference namely "Who are the worn-out preachers?" He meant who were unable to itinerate any more. Think on these things and write down your reflections.

Seventh Sunday of the Year

1/14/79

"Ask and it shall be given you. Seek and you will find. Knock and it shall be opened to you." —Matthew 7.7

We neglect our prayers because we are so occupied with the life of today with the whole family working. Prayer cannot be neglected without suffering real spiritual loss. Prayer teaches us to lean upon the Lord and cling to His promises. We need His blessed assurance and love. Paul tells us that God will supply all our needs through Jesus Christ our Lord.

Everyone should pray for each other. The Bible tells us how and where to pray and it provides a storehouse of illustrations, Jonah, we are informed, prayed under water, other Biblical persons prayed on mountain tops, others in the midst of battle, some in good times, some in bad times, some often, and some seldom. Wherever you may be, you can pray. Much of the Bible consists of prayers offered by people in every kind of circumstance.

Petitions addressed to God are as varied as the range of human imagination. There are prayers of adoration, confession, intercession, thanksgiving, supplication, and submission. Some are short, some long some in secret, some in public. In the New Testament there is one kind of prayer that is having a genuine revival today, prayer for each other. The early church believed that Christians should pray for each other—a person to person prayer.

In the book of Acts, we find that the Antioch church fasted, prayed, and laid hands on Paul and Barnabas before they left for the mission field. The elders of the church at Ephesus knelt on the beach at Miletus with Paul and prayed for him. We may pray for a lot of people or things and yet miss the boat by not praying for the person next to us who may need help desperately.

To meet this need and follow the New Testament pattern, Christians who are serious about prayer need to get together in groups and pray. When people pray for each other, beautiful things happen. Love comes to the surface, Jesus Christ becomes an immediately present Savior. The Holy Spirit becomes known as God Him self and it is amazing what happens when we follow His example. He said, "If my people who are called by my name, humble themselves, and pray and seek my face, and turn from their wicked ways, then I will hear from heaven and will forgive their sins, and will heal their land, and they will be my people and I will be their God."

4/25/71

"And the vessel he made of clay was marred in the hand of the potter, so he made it again another vessel as seemed good to the potter to make it. O house of Israel, cannot I do with you as this potter did, says the Lord." —Jeremiah 18.4-6

The unique service of religion is always the spiritual vision, not the contractor's blueprint, not the direction, but the dreams. The lesson that Jeremiah learned from the potter is strikingly modern. Jeremiah first found Israel as a nation held against the wheel in the grip of blind fate. He rejected this message. Then he saw Israel as a tragedy of a nation with whom God could do nothing. He rejected this also. Then he saw Israel as the opportunity of God to make her again.

This is then the deepest and final answer of religious faith to life. It is not that fate is against us, nor that we are made of material so stubborn and unyielding that nothing can be done with us. But rather, whatever our circumstances, by the grace of God we can be made again. No message that can be given to us from religion is more fundamental than this one.

From the wide areas of the social frontier to the inner recesses of our own baffled and fearful souls, no message is more important. What great power lies in the message that life can be made again. It is repentance to the sinner, and comfort to the burdened, and something dynamic to the disinterested. God's creative work is not over, it is still in the making. Whatever our condition may be spiritually, God is ready and willing to receive us if we humbly come to Him through faith.

He can make things again, yes even our dream of everlasting life can come true. Although God ordained Jeremiah to be a prophet even before he was born, Jeremiah made mistakes. Like Jeremiah we make mistakes. We are only human and need reassurance and redirection throughout our lives if we would want to spend everlasting life with our Savior.

Questions and Thoughts for Reflection

1. My grandfather was definitely a man of prayer. The only time I really got to hear him do it was at the dinner table, but it was clear it was such an important part of his life. Prayer of course is conversation with God, and like in any conversation it can involve asking things and telling things but it can also involve pleading and confessing. It involves all sorts of conversation. I was taught at an early age the JOY principle, namely Jesus, Others, and Yourself. That is prayers of adoration and intercession should come before "me" prayers. It is a good principle.

Some people say prayer changes things. I say God has chosen to use prayer to change things. Prayer is not a magical change agent, and it doesn't work like rubbing a magic lamp and making a wish. God is the change agent. There are exhortations in the Bible that encourage private prayer but also group prayer, the most famous of which is the so-called Lord's Prayer, but really it is the prayer Jesus gave as a pattern for His disciples.

Corporate prayer can sometimes go wrong. I remember an occasion when at the last minute at my uncle's house my father was asked to pray before we shared Thanksgiving dinner. He was a little flustered and said, "Dear Lord please pardon this food and bless our sins in Jesus' name, Amen." Needless to say, that produced some laughs and my aunt was frankly rather miffed, as she had worked so hard to prepare the good food. My father didn't soon live down that mistaken prayer. Have you recently evaluated your prayer life?

Do you know that God knows what you mean even when the words don't come out right? Do you realize that the point of prayer is not to inform God about something since He already knows, the point is communion with God through communication and being privileged to participate in God's plan and will for us all?

2. Once again my grandfather turns to Jeremiah 18 but this time it leads to a lesson about how God can remake us as needed, and so we should not give up on ourselves. We should not repeat the cliché "you can't teach old dogs new tricks" but rather believe that even in old age people can be changed for the better by God's grace. Perhaps you know a story of such a change. Have you ever shared it with your Bible study or in church or with friends? I remember doing a revival right after 9/11 and there were many people present. One was an older man with an old camcorder filming the revival. He was full of joy. The minister told me some were skeptical about him because he had been the town lothario and a heavy drinker who had been led to Christ by that minister. Even Christians become skeptical of people who change in later life, but is that the attitude we should have? Examine your own heart and see if you have made snap judgment about others in your church or work place. Ask yourself, do I really know that person's character, and even if so, have I forgotten Jesus can change them and died for them?

Eighth Sunday of the Year

9/19/71

"All Scripture is given by the inspiration of God and is profitable for doctrine, reproof, for correction, and for instruction in righteousness, that God's person may be perfect, thoroughly furnished unto all good works." —1 Timothy 3.16-17

The Scriptures indicate that the essential goal of life is to live, and to live worthily and properly. This indicates the mission of Jesus, the mission of humankind, and the meaning of religion. We should learn to live rightly and like it.

Literature has always been a great aid to proper living. The classics, the great novels, and the great poems have all contributed to our search for truth and for the right way of life. Literature has inspired humankind to be its best. Life expresses itself in literature, and literature should find its way back into life. In religious and Christian literature we find the source, basis, and motive for Christian living. Religious and Christian living produced the Bible, and the Bible serves its purpose as it finds expression in our lives. It is the "one inch bookshelf which meets the needs of life as no other literature can." But out of the Bible has grown the great companions of the heart, such as Augustine's *Confessions*, or the *Imitation of Christ*, or the smaller catechisms, and other well-known devotional books.

So, we should get inspiration as we read the greatest book on earth, yes the greatest literature—the Bible. And we do this so we may grow as Christians fulfilling our lives and God's purposes for us.

7/30/78

"What is man that thou art mindful of him?" —Psalm 8.4

Do you remember World War I, the Depression, World War II, Hitler's Germany killing millions of Jews, the atomic bomb dropped on Japan, and Vietnam where the leaders had whole villages destroyed because they said that was the only way they could save them? How about all the strife that is happening in the Middle East today? Then we ask—Why doesn't God stop all this conflict in the world? Our God is a God who has chosen to give His creatures freedom to choose their own way. This freedom makes human beings responsible moral agents that can say yes to God's purposes. That power of contrary choice can also be used to say no to God's plans. The existence of so much sin in the world shows how far human beings have gone wrong, astray from God's divine purposes.

Yet in some of the darkest hours of human history new light from God has manifested itself. God acted through Abraham, He acted through Moses, even though Moses failed so many times. He acted through men of faith like Gideon, courageous men like Amos, compassionate men like Hosea, men of trust like Barnabas, and men of faith like Paul.

Some theologians in the past have said God is dead. Others have used God in their emergencies and then forgotten Him. Some have tried to put God out of business, but failed. Yet human beings have found in nature, in the discoveries of science, and in God's Word, and even in our own experiences evidence of the reality of God and His involvement in our daily lives.

God's supreme act is when He came into the human sphere in the person of Jesus Christ. Jesus is God's ultimate and complete expression of Him self to humankind. God sent His message and His messengers into the world, and what is this message? "I have come that you may have life and have it abundantly." Yes, life in all its fullness. Jesus came into this life to call us back to a loving Father. Through the Holy Spirit this same message is communicated down through every generation. He wants us to follow Him and His example, for He went about doing good. Are you content with just going about, or are we going about doing good, showing we are His workmanship?

Questions and Thoughts for Reflection

1. Did you notice how the most famous New Testament passage about the inspiration and purpose of the Bible is about the Old Testament (there wasn't a New Testament yet when that verse was written) and did you notice the ethical function of Scripture? It's for training in righteousness! It's for urging us to do good works! It's for correction. Yes, it's also for training in basic theological beliefs as well. Sometimes Protestants have not properly emphasized the ethical thrust of much of Scripture or for that matter the necessity to do good works. After all, the ten commandments and also the great commandment not to mention the great commission are all mandates to *do something*, not merely to believe something. Do you emphasize to others that the Bible is a call to action as much or more than it is a call to contemplation and belief? As James stressed faith without works is dead. It is not a living faith, or as I like to put it real faith works. It does things. In 1 Corinthians 3 Paul reminds his audience that there is accountability for our deeds, and in particular our ministerial deeds, and there are rewards for serving the Lord well. Salvation itself is not a reward, it's a gift of grace, but did you know there are rewards in the Kingdom for serving well, not least of which is Jesus' own commendation: "Well done, good and faithful servant, inherit the Kingdom." Is that the one thing you most hope to hear when you arrive in His presence in heaven? I would hope so. Notice that verse for today talks about what we have done for the Lord, not if we have said "Lord, Lord" numerous times.

2. While the prosperity Gospel message (which is not really biblical) has suggested that God "wants you rich," this message frankly does not comport with Jesus' message to the rich young ruler, and a dozen other passages. So, what does it mean for a Christian today to live "the abundant life" which fulfills Jesus' promise that He came that we might have life and have it abundantly?

In the first place, Jesus is talking about everlasting life, life that goes on "unto infinity and beyond." The people He is talking to already have mundane life. He is talking about something more. It is of course natural in a hedonistic and materialistic culture to think Jesus is talking about more material possessions, but He is not. Indeed, the Sermon on the Mount only gives us the exhortation 'ask and it will be given to you' after Jesus has said that He will take care of our basic needs like He does even for the birds. Jesus is not interested in having a bunch of greedy hedonistic followers. He preaches the Gospel of "enough," the Gospel of self-sacrifice, not the Gospel of self-indulgence. My grandfather understood this perfectly well and deliberately lived a simple lifestyle, and a self-sacrificial one at that. As he says at the end of that lesson, abundant life has to do with a closer walk with God and sharing in God's life. Have you understood what the abundant life is really all about? Abundant life is not constituted by the abundance of your possessions.

Ninth Sunday of the Year

8/1/76

"How you have fallen from heaven, oh star of the morning [i.e., meaning the Devil]. You have been cut down to the earth, you who have weakened the nations, but you said in your heart, I will ascend to heaven, I will raise my throne above the stars of God. I will ascend above the heights of the clouds, I will make myself like the most High." —Isaiah 14.12-14

In this passage, the Prince of Hell, who stands behind the King of Babylon, declares his own motivation for encouraging humankind to rebel against God. The prophet quotes Satan's manifesto against God back in the primeval rebellion which he had led against God in heaven. Quite clearly Satan, as a free agent, had made up his mind to exalt himself above God and to choose his own will in preference to the known will of God. He who had been created by God attempted to dethrone God his creator. He should have known that the created cannot exalt himself above the Creator. Nevertheless, in the exercise of his own free will Satan did what you and I all of the fallen race of Adam do, apart from the redeeming grace of God. He put himself in first place, the place that belongs to God alone. Such is the deceitfulness of sin that it can impel us to attempt what our mind and reason could easily perceive to be impossible and altogether wrong.

Irrationality and absurdity lie at the very heart of sin. Under Satan's influence both Adam and Eve later repeated that same hopeless attempt. They put self-will and self-advantage above the known will of God the master and maker of the universe. We should be able to understand Satan's foolish egotism and pride, for we ourselves have been guilty of it.

When God created both Satan and Adam perfect, He included within that perfection, the power and responsibility of free-will, and this applies to us today. God is love and we must express and live out our love for Him. Without love there can be no meaningful relationship with God. Therefore, the possibility of rebellion and evil was indispensable for the creation of any moral agent, whether angel or human being. Jesus came to save that which is lost, which is to say all of us for all of us have offended and sinned against God and need repentance.

7/20/75: The Inborn Sense of Deity

"Then God said, 'Let us make humankind in our image, after our likeness.'" —Gen. 1.26

In the mind of every human being there exists a sense of God. It is there quite naturally. God Himself has placed an awareness of Himself in the whole universe and in every human heart. So when people neither honor nor consecrate their lives to his will they are condemned by their own testimony. There is no nation so barbarous or so savage that have not had implanted in them a persuasion that God exists. Never, since the beginning of the world, has there been any region, any city, or even any home without an object of worship. This in itself is a confession that the sense of God is inscribed on every heart.

It is ridiculous to say, as some do, that worship was invented by the cunning of a few individuals for the purpose of keeping the simple people in ignorance. Such people would not have succeeded anyway, as God had already imbued the minds of all persons with a conviction of His existence. The more unbelievers try to hide from the truth of God, the more the divine majesty beats on their hearts and consciences.

How do we know such a persuasion is inborn? No matter how furiously people wrestle with this fact, they are unable to extricate themselves from the fear of God. From this we can gather that a sense of Deity is not a doctrine to be learned in school, but one which we have had even before our birth. All people are endowed by the Creator with God consciousness, who never lets us forget Him, no matter how much we strive to do just that. All human beings are superior to other forms of life, because they know and worship God by which alone we can aspire to immortality and everlasting life.

Questions and Thoughts for Reflection

1. Free will? It's a subject well worth discussing. While I don't disagree that God created humans and angels with freedom of choice, the issue since the time of Adam is that human beings are experiencing a myriad of sinful inclinations and don't really have "free will" in the *absolute* sense any more. We could say that with the help of God's grace they can and do make at least some good choices, but this is not because they inherently have free will any more. It would be better to say they still have the power of contrary choice, and the decision is still in their hands, by the grace of God. They are not pre-programmed one way or another. This is precisely why God still holds sinners responsible for their choices and behavior. They cannot say "the Devil made me do it," and in regard to Christians themselves, as Romans. 8.1-4 says the Spirit has set them free from the rule or bondage of sin and death and so Paul can also say in 1 Cor. 10—'no temptation has overcome you that is not common to humanity, such that with the temptation God can provide an adequate means of escape.' Christians are supposed to live a life without excuses. Greater is He who is in us, than anything the world can tempt us with or throw at us. So, do you believe God's grace is sufficient so that you can choose to live a life that is pleasing to God and edifying to your fellow human beings?

2. A lot of times we make mistakes in our assumptions about the lost, for example we simply assume they are lost because they don't know anything about God, in part because they have not heard the Gospel. Romans 1.18-32 however suggests this notion is not entirely correct. For one thing, Paul reminds us that the reality of an all-powerful Creator God is present throughout His creation. So, it's not just a matter of "they are lost because they haven't heard the Gospel." Indeed, Paul insists in that passage that "though they know God, they

refuse to acknowledge God and exchange the truth about God for a lie." Now you can't exchange something you have never had, so Paul is saying they are lost chiefly because they have rejected what they do know of the true God, and exchanged that knowledge for various forms of idolatry and immorality—two things that go together. Bad belief readily leads to bad behavior. So Pop is quite right that we all have an innate sense that there is a God, and we as sinners quite naturally fear Him, or would like to banish Him from our thoughts and lives. Think for a minute about what the Psalmist says: "The fool says in his heart 'there is no God.'" Perhaps you have run into some folks like that. How would you go about convincing them otherwise? What biblical wisdom would you use?

Tenth Sunday of the Year

10/5/78

"No man is an island, entire of itself." —John Donne

I have heard the statement many times: "I don't depend on anybody for anything." People who believe that are very short-sighted. Where do our clothes come from, our food, our medicine? It would be hard to find out just how many people are involved in our lives! There is no such thing as a person being an island unto himself, dependent on no one else. A person may say I'll do what I want and it's nobody's business, but how far wrong can you be in a situation like this? There are no self-made persons. Everyone was born from another human being. And no one can pull themselves up by their own bootstraps without help or support from some others, or at least living in a situation and place where there is the freedom to do so.

Then too, a person never knows *how much* influence his life has on others. This is something we cannot control and often are ignorant of. Yes, we can control to some degree the kind of influence we have on others. Even the person who just sits down and does nothing has an influence on those they sit beside. You may ask—Can a Christian have a negative influence on others? Yes! A negative influence can happen by just not saying or doing anything. Whatever we do or fail to do has its influence on those around us. We may just refuse to take a stand or to speak for or against an issue that causes misunderstanding and causes a negative influence. There is such a thing as sins of omission, like when we fail to love our neighbor as ourselves. So, we don't have to do anything to be a negative influence on others. As the famous poem says, no man is an island, and I would add no man is an island even by being silent.

There is a danger in excess liberty. Paul has much to say about Christian liberty. A Christian can do many things that may not hurt him personally, but his example may lead others astray. We should not do things that create a stumbling block for others. Our liberty does not make us an island. We may have many opportunities to influence towards evil by indifference or by silence. A person's life should count for righteousness when it is governed by love. A person should love his fellow human beings and God enough to choose the best for his own life so that there will be a positive influence, whoever it impacts. When love prevails, no one's life is an island. Remember the first and second commandment to love our God with all we are and our neighbor as ourselves. When we remember the greatest commandment we can never see ourselves as totally independent or self-made persons.

10/25/81

"Until we all come unto a perfect man, unto the measure of the stature of the fullness of Christ." —Ephesians 4.13

An intelligent person does not work without an aim. God has a purpose for His universe. That purpose encompasses every part of the universe, including every individual person. And God has definitely told us what our portion is in that purpose. It is to come unto perfection.

Lest we misunderstand the ideal, He has defined perfection for us. It is the measure of the stature of the fullness of Christ, or as John phrases it "we shall be like Him." This doesn't indicate a standardization with all individuality purged out. On the contrary, John becomes a Christ-like John, and Peter a Christ-like Peter. Paul sums up both of the elements concerned in one trenchant statement—"Christ lives in me." Christ, in taking possession of Paul did not destroy the "me." Christ entered into him and lived in him manifesting Himself through it. God's purpose for us being our perfection, we ought to make that our purpose too. We should long for it, and strive for it. But we are not left alone to strive to achieve this humanly impossible goal, unaided. As Christ was both human and divine, so we, by receiving the Holy Spirit, become both human and partakers of the divine nature. And when the Holy Spirit will have wrought His completed work in us, then we shall be ready to be measured as complete work in Christ. He will present us faultless, with exceeding joy. Yes, God has a purpose for His universe and for humankind, so let us be prepared to do His will.

Questions and Thoughts for Reflection

1. The first lesson for this Sunday goes against the grain of much of the mythology that swirls around in a voluntaristic society like the one we have in America. There are all these Horatio Alger stories or Dale Carnegie stories about people who are "self-made men." This mythology has been further perpetuated in the writings of Ayn Rand who wrote about "The Virtues of Selfishness." I once saw an interview with an African American man in South Carolina who was turning 100. He was asked a lot of questions, and oddly the interview took place in front of what had been a plantation house. This interview took place in the 70s or 80s and the man was a child or grandchild of slaves. He was asked what he thought about folks whose ancestors had been slave owners. He replied succinctly "Until I see someone born with clothes on, I ain't gonna figure they are any more than me." That's exactly right. We were all created equal, equally bearing the image of God, equally persons of sacred worth, and NONE of us are self-created, self-made human beings. We all need each other. John Donne goes on to say in his famous poem, "Any man's death diminishes me, for I am a part of mankind. Therefore, do not ask for whom the bell tolls, it tolls for thee." We are inherently dependent on each other, need each other, and are called to love each other.

But what is the difference between understanding all this and having an unhealthy co-dependency on one or more persons when we should be mature individuals without becoming individualists? Paul provides us with a clue in Galatians 6 when in the space of the first few verses in that chapter he says both: "bear one another's burdens and so fulfill the law of Christ" and, in the next breath, "let each person carry their own load." On the surface, that sounds like a contradiction but it isn't. We all need help with burdens from time to time, but we all are also called upon to do our own part in life and not expect others to do what we are capable of and called to do. How should these things be balanced in your view?

2. What's the difference between being Christ, and being Christ-like? I like what my grandfather says in this sentence: "This doesn't indicate a standardization with all individuality purged out. On the contrary, John becomes a Christ-like John, and Peter a Christ-like Peter." As he adds, when Paul speaks of "Christ in me" there is still the "me" in whom Christ has taken up residence. So, we do not become gods, or God, we become Christ-like.

This is one of the places where traditional Mormon teaching has gone terribly wrong. Our goal is not to become gods. Indeed, that was the temptation offered to Adam and Eve in the garden by the powers of darkness. And in any case, when Paul calls us to Christ-likeness, he is not calling us to develop a God complex or savior mentality. He is calling us to model our *behavior* and moral outlook on Christ's. Inwardly we are being transformed day by day into a more Christ-like character, all being well. So, what does 'work out your salvation with fear and trembling as God works in you to will and to do' mean in your life? Have you made progress in the past year in your sanctification? Are you a more loving, a more kind, a more patient person than you were previously?

Eleventh Sunday of the Year

9/14/69

"In the beginning God created the heavens and the earth . . ."
"All things were made by him and without him not anything was made." —Genesis 1.1; John 1.1

God has been in the space business for a long time. The heavens declare the glory of God says the Psalmist. According to the Apostle Paul, God's Son, Jesus Christ is the one who maintains the celestial bodies in their courses. The moon has been glorifying its Creator for all time simply by being the moon, by rotating around the earth and moving the tides that give us life as we know it. God gave human beings dominion over the material world. Man has now walked on the moon and more recently he has seeded the hurricanes with silver iodine crystals from about 3,500 feet high. The eye of one of these hurricanes was about 15 miles wide after the seeding process. The eye was expanded to about 40 miles in diameter, which lessened the intensity of the storm to a great extent. Human beings have had great success in exploring God's creation. But the real problem is not human accommodation to its environment but rather human accommodation to itself. Humankind has not known too much difficulty in subduing the earth. Yet humans have had enormous difficulty in subduing themselves.

To go to the moon was no insoluble problem for us. But to learn to humble our pride, to control our lusts, to love our neighbors—all our neighbors that order seems to be more than humankind can manage. Jesus Christ is God's provision to meet human need at this point. On the cross of Calvary Jesus bore our sins and solved the human equation by giving us new life. How much greater it is to fill our lives with Christ rather than our bag with moon rocks. "For what shall it profit a man that he gain the whole world and lose his soul." All worldly success counts for nothing if we do not have Christ in our hearts. He has said He will return to hold us accountable for the deeds we have done in the body. Will we be ready for His coming?

7/27/69

"See then that you walk circumspectly, not as fools but as wise redeeming the time, because the days are evil." —Ephesians 5.15-16

When Paul wrote this, did he mean we must save time? No, but that is one of our modern obsessions, we even talk about labor and time saving devices. We are always saving time, and yet so many seem to have no time for anything, at least, nor for the things that make life really worth living. They have no time to read a book, or to cultivate a friendship, or to spend an hour in the worship of God. The question of how to save time and when, and the worthwhile uses to which it may be put, are seldom a subject most people even take time to think about. But why bother saving time unless you can use it to redeem life of some of its ills? The very term to redeem means to rescue or to relieve, to liberate from bondage. Does our modern idea of saving time do this, or does it lay fresh burdens upon us?

What is time anyway? The scientist tells me that time is a convenient method by which the mind notes certain recurrent motions in space. Every moment of our astronauts was timed even to when they first set foot on the moon. The philosopher says time is a moment of consciousness between two eternities, the past and the future. The Bible states that one day with the Lord is as a thousand years, and a thousand years as one day. Human beings work by the clock, God works by love. It is true that the happy person is the one who spends his time benefiting his fellow human beings by Christian activity. For him time flies, which in one sense means he is becoming like God.

Human beings have accomplished great things. Who every thought we would walk on the moon? But then let us reflect on the fact that God made the moon, and He alone gives us the right to be sons and daughters of God. We can only do what God permits us to do. Without God, there would be no moon and no man. Without God there is no past, or present or future, no everlasting life for us. So, the question becomes—are we allotting our time wisely or foolishly?

This is a serious question and I mean it spiritually, morally, and even nationally. Are we fulfilling our obligations in life or are we apathetically drifting with the tide. Life and time are of the utmost importance, but love is the most important element in our material life. If we have the right sort of love, all our human troubles will resolve themselves.

Time, when passed, can never be recalled. As the old saying goes—time and tide wait for no one. Yesterday is gone forever. Whatever we did or failed to do cannot be retrieved, or recaptured. We are all aware, perhaps painfully, perhaps gleefully of the changes that are wrought by the passage of time, and that ultimately time will bring us to that same place in the scenario of life where we will be weighed, balanced, judged or otherwise evaluated according to some immutable law or perhaps according to our own accomplishments in this life.

Does anyone on this earth really know what will happen to them beyond that point in time? This question is not raised for the purpose of arguing the philosophies of truth, of religions, of faiths or beliefs, but merely to point out that each of us would perhaps be wise to give more thought to the subject of time and make some evaluations of what the term means to us as individual persons. There are perhaps thousands of ways of evaluating time and it can mean many things to many people. A baby has no concept of time. The child, the adolescent, the young adult generally act as if they will live forever. Many people refuse to recognize the inevitability of the passage of time and what it will do to them Then suddenly a person attains the age of 40 or 50 and begins to think where has the time gone—half or more of my life is gone so how much more time do I have? What will I do with it? Is it time I thought about time?

We should not wait until too much time has passed to start evaluating and using time wisely and frankly it is when we are young that is the ideal time to plan our time in life. I am reminded of the old quote by Whittier—"the saddest words of tongue or pen, what might have been, what might have been." We know that there are no firm answers to time but rather we have the hope that each of us will be stimulated to dwell with beneficial contemplation on the subject of time. As legend has it, we know what time has wrought, but we do not know what time will bring. How much time do we set aside for worship or for prayer?

Our consciousness has been seared with the knowledge that all things worldly have a beginning and an end. Our lives are bracketed by twin moments of birth and death. Our days dawn and set. We have come to know that time and its passage is a relentless motion and is representative of the constancy and reliability of a great universal law. Lest we think we are at the mercy of time, I would remind us all that there is one outside of and over time—God. Thanks to God, who in His wisdom has decreed that in due time, in the midst of the darkest night, through our own labors we shall pick up the candle and rekindle the light of understanding and love, and presage a new and more glorious day when we will be with our Maker forever.

Questions and Thoughts for Reflection

1. The first lesson for this Sunday is about putting things in perspective. When even the walking on the moon is compared to things of everlasting significance, our greatest human achievements seem miniscule compared to what God has accomplished as the Creator of the universe and the Redeemer of humankind. As my grandfather suggests, subduing the earth and exploring the solar system seems to be easier than subduing our own human problems—war, prejudice, hatred, inhumanity and much more. It is interesting that the Psalmist in Psalm 8 looks at the universe and asks, "What is man that thou art mindful of him?" And yet God looks at human beings and wants to have special love relationships with them. God appreciates His creation and calls it good, but He cherishes and loves humanity and seeks to redeem and restore them. If you were to list the greatest accomplishments in human history what would you list? Would you mention the seven ancient wonders of the world? The only one that is still standing is the pyramids in Egypt. Or would you remember

that cross on Golgotha and that single event which changed human history forever? What is your perspective on what really matters?

2. It is clear from reading all these lessons that my grandfather had done a lot of reflection on the meaning of time for the time being—humans. Animals are not worried about the clock, and even the higher primates don't wear watches. It's human beings that are obsessed with time. Furthermore, since with God one day is as a thousand years, and vice versa (see 2 Peter 3.8) clearly human beings don't seem to view time the way God does. We are not on God's standard time. But should we be? Since our time on earth is limited, shouldn't we learn how to use time wisely, never wasting it, and even find out what "redeeming the time" means, which surely has something to do with using it in a way that glorifies God and edifies our fellow human beings? And certainly, God does not want us to obsess about time. The past is irretrievable, and the future is in God's hands—and He is simply not going to disclose when His Son will return. As Mark 13.32 reminds us, during His earthly ministry even Jesus could say that in regard to the timing of that event, no one knows, not even the Son only the Father. That fact should have put an end to human predictions about the Second Coming. All such predictions so far have had an 100% failure rate. Isn't it time we learned that prognostications are an all too human attempt to control the future? So, I would say God reveals enough about the future to give us hope and great expectations, but not so much that we don't have to live by faith every day. What do you think about that suggestion?

Twelfth Sunday of the Year

10/26/80

"He has made known his ways unto Moses, his acts unto the children of Israel." —Psalm 103.7

In the Old Testament it is stated that the secret of the Lord is with those that fear Him. That is one of the greatest verses in the Bible. But how much more wonderful are the words of Christ when He declares, "I will love him, and manifest myself to him." Even in our age, a close walk with God will bring a knowledge of God's ways that will help us understand things which cause many to doubt and fear. Mysteries must always remain, but any sense of being puzzled by some irresponsible Supreme Being will be banished. Yet we must remember that obedience to God is the key that makes possible for us as an entry into God's inner purposes. "If anyone will do his will," states our Lord to His disciples, "he shall know the doctrine." Our main trouble is not external because of the things that happen around us, but rather internal because of our unwillingness to accept God's will and identify ourselves with God's great purposes.

In the light of God's countenance, you will be illumined within and will see God's light on your pathway must be the way that God has chosen for you. On that road He can and will make known to you His ways, His deeper inner purposes for you His child and for His world. Prayer is the greatest and fastest communication we can use today. For God has said, and it will come to pass "before they call, I will answer and while they are yet speaking, I will hear." We know His ways but do we follow them? Yes, He knows our future before it happens, but through His love we can be saved from our sins. He will redeem us if we will only do His will. The answer is ours.

8/30/70

"That by two immutable things in which it is impossible for God to lie, that we might have a strong consolation who have fled for refuge to lay hold of the hope set before us."
"For I am the Lord, I change not." —Hebrews 6.18; Malachi 3.6

It is impossible for God to be inconsistent. This truth should impress human hearts and be constantly before them. There are five implications: 1) God cannot fail to be holy. The sinner is dealing with a being who is consistently holy in every demand. 2) God cannot fail to enforce His Law. Having given the moral Law to humankind, He cannot disregard nor set it aside. He must hold all fully accountable and He cannot do otherwise. This should alarm transgressors. 3) God cannot admit sin into heaven. Sin defiles, sin is anarchy. Sin is the transgression of the Law. It is also the disposition to transgress. It is therefore impossible for God ever to admit unregenerated people into heaven. 4) God cannot save anyone without repentance. In infinite wisdom God made a plan of salvation. That plan requires repentance. Jesus said, "unless you repent you shall all likewise perish." "No one comes to the Father, except by me." This is true by the very nature of God. He so loved the world that He gave His Son as the Redeemer and He cannot be untrue to His Son by saving some on the basis of some other plan. 5) God cannot fail to save those who come to Him in His appointed way. Those who repent of their sins and trust in Christ are surely, inevitably, and eternally saved.

God will be true to every promise, otherwise the whole Bible would be a farce. God is truth and He cannot be otherwise. We know His plan and His commandments. The burden is entirely upon us. We must give Him complete command of our lives. He has said the wages of sin is death. Everlasting life should be the goal of every human being.

Questions and Thoughts for Reflection

1. It may seem obvious but if you want to know God's will for your life, you need to know God. The ways, even some of the secrets, of

God are known by those who revere Him. If you want to understand God's purposes for your life, then you need to move on faith and trust God like Abraham did, even when he didn't yet know where he was going or would end up. As it has been said, it is easier to steer a ship in the right direction when it is already moving. Our faith and trust are not based on what we do not know about God but rather on what we have come to know about Him. Corrie Ten Boom tells the story of being in Ravensbruck concentration camp with a Jewish woman who was a concert violinist. Horribly, when a death camp guard found this out about the woman he deliberately broke several of the fingers on her playing hand. Corrie would regularly talk to the other women where she was about God's love, and finally the Jewish lady had had enough. She showed Corrie her bent fingers and said, "How can you believe in a God of love who would allow this to happen to my fingering hand?" Corrie's reply was honest: "I do not know why this tragedy has happened, but my faith is not based on what I do not understand about God and life's tragedies. It's based on what I do know—'No pit or problem is so deep that God's love is not deeper still.'"

This answer has helped me personally during difficult times in my life. Our daughter Christy died suddenly of a pulmonary embolism at thirty-two. One minute she was here with us celebrating my sixtieth birthday, and only a few days later she was found dead in her apartment in Durham, North Carolina, with her two dogs lying beside her. We never could understand why this had happened right when her life was going well and she had a wonderful job with IBM. Perhaps someday we will understand better, but what we do know was having her in our lives for thirty-two years was a blessing, and so we decided we would celebrate the time we had with her, rather than bemoan the sudden loss. We were not owed more time with Christy. Our time with her was always a gift, not a right. I suspect that if we would look at life as a gift from God rather than a right, many of the mysteries would not seem so important. So, is your faith based on what you do know about God? Do you know Him well enough to know His plans for us are for good and not for harm? God's will is both easier to understand and easier to accept if we know Him well enough to know He loves us and wants the best for us.

2. God does not change. He is the same yesterday, today, and tomorrow. All human beings change over time, some for the better, some not. Furthermore, God's Word is as unchanging and reliable as He is. When He tells us something we can know it is true. He doesn't make promises He can't or won't keep. Now some of God's promises are conditional in nature. Notice how this sentence starts: "If my people, who are called by my name, repent and turn back to me, then . . . I will bless them." But what if those people do not repent? What if they choose to turn their backs on their God? Well then God is under no obligation to do what He promises if they did repent.

Some Christians have mistakenly thought that God's Word works automatically, regardless of the human response. But often that is simply not the case. We are in a relationship with God, and some things are contingent on the state of that relationship, and in particular on whether we are responding properly to God's Word, His prophecies, His promises at least in so far as our getting to personally benefit from those promises and dictates. This is not because some external factors or circumstances can get in the way of an almighty God's will being done. It is because we ourselves are being related to by God as persons, not as pieces to be moved around on a divine chess board. And as persons we have choices about how we respond to God's commands, requests, promises. The situation is interactive and God wants us to freely respond in love and trust to what He requires of us.

There is a reason the Lord's prayer includes the petition, "thy will be done on earth as it is in heaven." God's will is *not* always and automatically done on earth. Much depends on the human response. So, the question for us is, Are we listening closely enough to God's Word and then acting in obedience on it so that His will can be done in and through us? Are we indeed, as Paul once suggested, co-workers with God in His plans of redemption? Are we His emissaries and agents, or are we not?

Thirteenth Sunday of the Year

Easter

"On the first day of the week, very early in the morning, the women took the spices they had prepared and went to the tomb. They found the stone rolled away from the tomb, but when they entered, they did not find the body of the Lord Jesus. While they were wondering about this, suddenly two men in clothes that gleamed like lightning stood beside them. In their fright the women bowed down with their faces to the ground, but the men said to them, 'Why do you look for the living among the dead? He is not here; he has risen! Remember how he told you, while he was still with you in Galilee: "The Son of Man must be delivered over to the hands of sinners, be crucified and on the third day be raised again."' Then they remembered his words."
—Luke 24.1-8

Very early on Sunday morning, the women went to the grave carrying spices they had prepared. They found the stone rolled away and the entrance to the tomb was thus open, so they went in, but the body of Jesus was gone. They were puzzled about this, when suddenly two men in bright shiny clothes appeared before them. The women were fearful and bowed down and the men said to them, "Why are you looking among the dead for one who is alive?" Then the Lord suddenly appeared to them and commissioned them to go tell the male disciples He was arisen.

After that, Jesus went to where those disciples were locked in a room for fear of the Jewish authorities. Jesus entered the room and said "peace be with you." Some were afraid perhaps because they thought they were seeing a ghost. Then Jesus said "Why are you troubled, why do you have doubts, look at my hands and side. It is me. Feel where the nails were and you will know that a ghost doesn't have flesh and bones, but you see I do."

Jesus offered to Thomas the opportunity to put his fingers where the nails had been and where the spear had pierced His side. The text does not say he did so. It says he knelt and said "My Lord and my God," which ironically is what the Emperor had asked to be called when the worship of the Emperor and the Emperor cult got going in the first century AD. But standing before the disciples was the risen Lord and the real God, the reality of what the Emperor was a mere grotesque parody.

Then the disciples believed and were filled with joy. Surprisingly, Jesus asked them if they had anything to eat there, and they handed Him a piece of cooked fish and He ate it then and there. Then He reminded them that He had told them about these events before He had been taken to the cross, and that everything written down about Him in the books of Moses, the writings of the prophets, and the Psalms had come true. Jesus conditioned their minds so they would now understand the Scriptures in light of Him and His ministry. He stressed, "it is written that the messiah must suffer and rise from the dead on the third day, and that in my name the message of repentance and forgiveness of sins must be preached to all the nations beginning in Jerusalem. You are my witnesses of all these things. I myself will send upon you what my Father has promised, but you must wait here until the power is given to you."

Remember that Jesus had said earlier to Martha, "I am the resurrection," not merely I give the resurrection but I am the resurrection. To come in contact with Jesus, and especially the risen Jesus is to come in contact with resurrection and everlasting life. Paul promises that some day those who are in Christ will be fully conformed to the image of Christ by means of resurrection. Then it will be absolutely true that we have become like the one we imitated and admired throughout our earthly life.

THIRTEENTH SUNDAY OF THE YEAR

"Let not your hearts be troubled." —John 14.1

These are the opening words of Jesus's great farewell message to His disciples. We find this theme again in John 15–16. We believe it to be true that Jesus spoke these very words, as is the case with all His other words, and they were intended for His people in all ages, as well as for His immediate audience of disciples. The ground for an untroubled heart is a firm belief in God. "You believe in God," said Jesus, "Believe also in me." Because God is, we can still believe that whatever the ravages of sin on earth, that through the ages one increasing purpose carries on. It is a divine purpose, for God has not lost control of His world. Notwithstanding the existence of sin and suffering and disobedience to His will, His purposes are moving on to ultimate triumph. We can rest confidently in the assurance of our Lord's presence in our midst now and always for "I have overcome the world."

Jesus never promised His people would have easy or smooth sailing in life. The early Christians suffered in ways we have never been called upon to suffer. They were not turned from the way because of persecutions or even martyrdoms. They held fast in the midst of all these tribulations to the promise Jesus had made—"Lo, I am with you always." The heart that is faithful therefore can be untroubled in the midst of the vicissitudes and contrary winds, knowing that God is all powerful and all love and compassion towards those He calls His own.

This is so because the heart that is stayed on Him and His love is able to rise above the circumstances of daily life. No outward storm can disturb the inward peace that He gives to those who trust in Him. Is there cause for your heart to be troubled today? Are the things you do and say acceptable in His sight? Could He say to you today, "well done, good and faithful servant; enter into the joy of your Lord"? How wonderful it would and will be to be with Him always.

Questions and Thoughts for Reflection

1. How do we view Easter? Are we prepared for it when it comes every Spring? Or is it as much of a shock to our systems as it was

to the disciples on that first Easter morning? The women who went to the tomb weren't expecting to encounter a risen Jesus. They had brought oil and spices to anoint the body and retard the smell of the decaying corpse, so the body could be visited for a week or more after Jesus' death. They were in shock and in mourning. They did not expect Jesus to overcome even death. This raises the question, Do we indeed believe Jesus rose bodily from the grave and do we understand the world-changing implications of that event? Do we actually realize that God's yes to life is louder than death's no? Sometimes in life we have some crucial teaching which we somehow miss the significance of. We don't store it away in our hearts and ponder it. And when later events suddenly confirm that the teaching was true and accurate, we are surprised. This was the exact condition of the disciples both women and men on Easter morning. Jesus had warned them He was going to die a violent death and then rise again, but somehow that teaching just didn't sink in, didn't register. Are there aspects of the Easter message that you have not fully grasped? Or do you celebrate Easter as merely a nice family get together? Or are you like our Greek orthodox friends who on Easter morning go running through the streets of Athens clanging pots and pans and saying "Christos aneste"—Christ is risen, He is risen indeed? Now is the time for you to really and fully grasp the miracle that is Easter and its implications for you.

2. It is normal for our hearts to be troubled and to be upset when bad things keep happening, not merely in general in the world, but more specifically to us in particular. But Jesus in the Farewell Discourses provides some good assurance to His disciples and the essence of it is "I have overcome the world." Notice He does not say, "I won't let the world trouble you or hurt you." As my grandfather points out, many early Christians were martyred and remained faithful unto death. Jesus never promised that no bad things will ever happen to His followers. Rather He promises He will be with them through it all. He promises that they, like He Himself, will overcome all those troubles and even death will not have the last word about a Christian's life. Have you ever spent time thinking about how to be an

overcomer in this troubled world? What does it mean to you personally that Jesus has promised both that He has overcome the world's troubles and that He will be with us through it all?

Fourteenth Sunday of the Year

3/31/68

"God is love." —1 John 4.8

There are about sixty places in the New Testament that refer to love, the love of God for His children. Sincere love could revolutionize the world and make it a heaven on earth. We don't really live until we know how to love with a divine or eternal love. You don't know how to love or to really live until you have daily contact with the God who is love and is life itself. The love the New Testament is speaking about is the opposite of hate, it involves being humble not arrogant, it knows how to give and not expect to receive, it knows how to forgive and love those who despitefully use you.

The Greeks coined a word—*agape*. It refers to unselfish love, even divine love, not merely brotherly love. It is a love expressed towards others without any ulterior motives. It is a love that puts the other person first without counting the cost. The human condition of fallen humanity is not capable of creating this sort of love. It's origin and source is the heart of God. A person can receive it from God, and then return it to God or share it with others.

Words of love are not always sufficient since action must go with them, then we having loving service. This requires both faith in God and faith in your fellow human beings. We accept that love is the great unifying power in the world. We agree that everything beautiful in this world is seasoned with love, the love for God and for each other. But when will we share such love? When we opened up our hearts to the perfect love of God that casts out all fear, then we can let it flow from us to others. John goes on to say "he that loves not, knows not God, for God is love." Even just knowing a God who is love requires love. Concern for others is not enough. Love in action, drawing on the divine love in our hearts is what is required to make a difference in the world. The words charity (*caritas*) and love mean practically the same thing. It refers to the greatest sort of caring in action.

Love is perhaps the most powerful and the most used word in our vocabulary but also the most misused. We say we love this or that referring to things, but a person can't really love things. Even worse we "love" or covet things and use people to get them, when we are supposed to love people and use things to help them, to provide for them. Unselfish love is when we love someone despite their flaws and faults, and regardless of material circumstances without counting the cost. If there was enough of the divine sort of love in the world there might not be any wars, any need for police or armies, or the FBI. Love could solve most of our problems in this world. Even some of the commandments of God would be unnecessary and become defunct if we really loved God with our whole heart and our neighbor properly.

And then there is the matter of forgiveness. Jesus told Peter he must do it seven times seventy if need be, if the offender asks for such forgiveness. Interestingly, the only other time the number seven times seventy shows up in Scripture is in the story of Lamech who vows to take revenge that many times for a wrong done to him. Jesus is thus reversing the curse that leads to violence and revenge by placing forgiveness as a solvent into a rock-hard heart. This is a very different matter than the abuses the word love has taken in recent years. Love is even used as an excuse for permissive or even promiscuous behavior! Some have distorted so-called "love" of their fellow human beings as an excuse for everything from riots to arson.

Without real love, I am nothing, you are nothing, and the world is nothing says St. Paul in 1 Corinthians 13, the ode to love. Love is basic to health, to success, or even just to a useful life. In fact, a person can wither and die without love, including love for himself as well as for God and others. To say one will perish without love does not mean that everyone without adequate love dies. Yet many do, for without love the will to go on living is often impaired, and leads to death.

Mostly, the lack of love makes people depressed, anxious, and without zest for life. They are lonely and unhappy without friends or work. Their lives are stripped of all creative activity and joy. But to love others, you must first love yourself. If you don't love yourself you can hardly expect to love others. The Bible states this plainly: "Thou shalt love thy neighbor as you love yourself." While this is not a *command* to love yourself, it assumes that you should and will do so. It has been said many times that love does not really exist until you give it away.

Furthermore, love is no virtue until you and I can love the unlovable. Then it becomes a virtue. What credit is it to merely love those who love you? Even pagans do that. Giving does not become a virtue until you and I can pardon the unpardonable. Some people really have an unlimited capacity for love. This is what Christianity teaches, and we should be conscious of the "last" and lasting commandment—"love one another, for to truly love one another is to love God as well."

7/14/68

"Train up a child in the way that he should go, and when he is old he will not depart from it." —Proverbs 22.6

In the springtime, the beautiful fields of grain, the trees in the orchard, and the flowers in the park come not by chance. Weeds however grow everywhere and grow without care, with little moisture. But who wants weeds? What can you do with weeds? They are an endless source of trouble. They not only mar the landscape but hinder the growth of the beautiful and useful as well. So too do the weeds in our lives. The choicest flower in the garden of life does not just happen by chance.

Abraham Lincoln once said, "All that I am and all that I ever hope to be, I owe to my darling mother." But in our day too many mothers and fathers are too busy with other things to give attention to the spiritual growth and development of their children. They take all that and more for granted. Some parents send their children to Sunday school, but they themselves never go, perhaps not even to church at all. Is it any wonder that some nasty weeds are growing in unexpected places? How refreshing to read what Paul said about the early training of Timothy: "I call to remembrance the unfeigned faith that is in you, which dwelled first in your grandmother Lois, and your mother Eunice." Truly many heartaches could have been avoided if fathers and mothers had sown the seed of the Word of God and daily watered it with earnest fervent prayer.

The wonderful service that Timothy rendered in that distant yesterday, our children will remember in their day, but not by accident. The seed must be sown if there is to be a harvest. What has happened to family love between parents and children? A child needs love and spiritual guidance if he would be a good person, never mind a good Christian person. With all the participation by many young people of today in immorality, dope addiction, and other things contrary to the right way of life, it becomes clear there has been a breakdown in family relations and instructions of the young. And in this the parents have failed their children and are greatly to be blamed for their children's misbehavior. The Bible says "faith, hope, and love, these three abide, but the greatest of these is love." These are the very foundations of the Christian home. Without them there is no Christian family or Christian home.

Questions and Thoughts for Reflection

1. One of the constant themes of my grandfather's lessons is love, but he is not talking about *eros*, the usual subject of modern conversation, he is talking about *agape* which comes from God. One of the more profound things said in the first lesson for today is that without love you cannot truly know God, for God is love. Notice that 1 John 4 does not say God is loving, though that is true. It says He is the very definition of love. If you were to sing the familiar chorus "I want to know what love is," the response should be consider God Himself. Too often we associate love with particular kinds of human feelings. But even a moment's reflection will show that this is not

what the great commandment to love God and love neighbor is talking about. You cannot command your feelings. You cannot say to yourself, I'll have warm mushy feelings all day, and thereby make it happen. Feelings come and go and are subject to all sorts of circumstances and situations—namely they are affected by one's health, by whether or not one is in a safe place and not dominated by fear, and so on. God is commanding love in action, and He shows what He means by giving His only begotten Son to live and die so that we might have everlasting life. At the heart of *agape* love is self-sacrificial service, whether one has accompanying positive feelings about it or not. What would you say is the cost of associating love with certain kinds of feelings all the time in our culture? One consequence is the lament we hear all too often "the thrill is gone out of our relationship, therefore we must not love each other anymore." What do you make of the saying perfect love casts out all fear, and we might add all hate as well? You cannot claim you love God if in fact you also hate your neighbor. Jesus made clear that loving God and neighbor is a single commandment. They go together. Think on these things.

2. One of the great concerns of my grandfather was the dissolution of the traditional family structure, including the failure of parents to "train up their children in the way that they should go." He blamed the desire for a more luxurious lifestyle in part for both parents feeling that they must be employed full time outside the home. What do you think of this diagnosis of what was going wrong with family life? Of course, he knew that sometimes, even with parents' best efforts to raise their children in a proper Christian way, things don't always turn out for the best. The proverb quoted in this lesson is a "truism" which means it is true often enough that the generalization is warranted but it is not some sort of claim that it is always and automatically true if parents raise their children right. In your view what does raising one's children in a proper Christian way entail these days? Does it require a stay-at-home mother or father, particularly during a pandemic, or at least a stay-at-home extended family member (say a grandparent)? How would you characterize what is best in these matters?

Fifteenth Sunday of the Year

11/24/68

"Giving thanks to God always for all things . . ." —Ephesians 5.20

A person must be impressed by the many instances of Jesus giving thanks. When He fed the five thousand He took the loaves, and when He had given thanks, He distributed them to the disciples, and the disciples distributed them to the crowd sitting down. When the four thousand were fed, He took the seven loaves and the fishes and gave thanks. At the grave of Lazarus, Jesus lifted up His eyes, and said, "Father, I thank you that you have heard me." Jesus humbly and reverently thanks His Father for the supplying of our every need.

We praise God for the miracles, but Jesus looks deeper and rejoices to find in the heart faith and love and thanksgiving. As He draws near Calvary, and the weight of the world's sin begins to bear down upon Him, with what tenderness and love He returns thanks both at the Passover feast and later as He institutes the Lord's Supper. Visualize these same disciples as they later gather with the brothers and sisters at the Lord's Table. Now they know the meaning of Calvary and the empty tomb. The tears flow but they have resurrection life and joy in their hearts as they look forward to eternity with Him. No wonder that Paul bursts forth with "thanks be unto God for his unspeakable gift."

Let us thank God for His unfailing, tender, loving care. Then let us live in the knowledge that we know that in everything God works for good for those who love Him, who are called according to His purpose. Then let us bank on the fact that our God will supply our every need according to His riches in glory in Christ Jesus. And let us be thankful, always for everything and for each other.

6/13/82

"Before Abraham was, I Am." —John 8.58

Older people were inclined to be jealous of young people. Some Jews thought that because Jesus was not fifty years old or more, He was too young to know anything. They also thought that older minds were inclined to be suspicious of young ideas. If a thing had never been done or thought it should never be done. Such was the instinctive reaction in a senior-dominated culture. There is a reason why the leaders who met in the city gates to make decisions were called "elders." They were older men, and no women were allowed to be in that group.

Galileo was persecuted, Jenner was ostracized. Edison was told his electric lights would burn down the house. Radio at first seemed the dream of madmen. In science, in politics, everywhere the new idea was suspect. This conservative approach was not without value, for new ideas should run the gauntlet of questions and testing.

When the older men criticized Jesus for His youth, He made no attempt to conciliate His critics. Instead, He said a totally unexpected and amazing thing—"Before Abraham was, I Am," or in effect, "Abraham may be old, but I am older! Nay, older and yet younger. Those things do not apply to me, for I am timeless. I was before the beginning of the world and will be after the end of the world." When His hearers recovered from what He said sufficiently, they tried to stone Him for His impudence.

The Gospel is timeless. We can think of it as both young and old. There is an undying youth in it which forever sends it out on new paths of conquest. Always it abandons old methods and concepts for better ones. When some Jews invoked Abraham in refutation of Jesus they forgot that Abraham was the greatest adventurer in Hebrew history. We can think of this Gospel as old because there is in it the truth which human beings have sought from the dawn of time. And yet we can think of it as new as well, for the mercies of God are new every morning.

Questions and Thoughts for Reflection

1. One of the things I was taught when young was called "thanks living." That is, I was taught that what Paul meant was that in all circumstances we should thank God for many things. We should develop an attitude of gratitude. I don't think Paul meant we should thank God FOR everything, because of course some things are sinful and evil. I cringe when I hear someone say "I thanked God for my cancer, even though it is killing me" based on a misunderstanding of what Paul was saying in this verse in Ephesians. Paul is talking about always giving thanks, even under bad circumstances for positive benefits already received from Christ. The previous context makes clear the sense of this all the way back to the thanksgiving section in Ephesians 1.

It is right, as my grandfather pointed out, that Jesus spent much of His prayer time giving thanks to God on numerous different sorts of occasions. When one's life, especially one's prayer life, is characterized primarily by thanksgiving, rather than constant petitions for God to give this or that or the other, it really changes one's view of life itself.

The story is told about a farmer who was just never pleased with much of anything and was always finding fault. He asked his wife to fix him two eggs for breakfast, one scrambled and one sunny side up. When his wife brought him his breakfast as he asked, he still had a scowl on this face. Exasperated, his wife said, "What's wrong now?" The farmer said, "You scrambled the wrong egg." Giving thanks for the good things one does have, rather than complaining about what one doesn't have, has to do with one's basic posture or attitude about life. Do you live life day to day with an attitude of gratitude? Or have you mistakenly developed a sense of entitlement? That whole orientation has in recent decades simply poisoned our public discourse. So let me be clear—life is a gift, not a right, blessings from God are all grace, not something owed to us. Evaluate your basic orientation to life and ask which orientation characterizes your attitude—gratitude or entitlement?

2. Unlike the culture in which Jesus lived, we live in a culture that idolizes youth. There are even numerous products on the market meant to make old people look younger, but unfortunately most them are rather like putting lipstick on a pig. The overall effect doesn't really improve one's appearance. In our culture, seniors are neglected, ignored, sometimes unnecessarily put in nursing homes so younger people won't have to take care of them. Fighting back, organizations like the AARP have had to be created for seniors to not be taken advantage of. Whereas the Bible teaches us to respect our elders, and even "revere the hoary head" our culture goes completely in the opposite direction, having "talent" shows on TV where overwhelmingly we are presented with very young people, some of whom are not even teenagers yet, over whom we are supposed to lavish praise. We even talk about "spoiling" our children and grandchildren, as if spoiling was a good thing. My grandfather points out that the Gospel, like God is timeless. The Gospel is never out of date, or out of time. Indeed, one could say it is both the old, old story, and yet the newest story of all because it keeps changing lives day by day. What is your perspective on old and young, on ancient and new? Have you let our culture's fixation on the young make you pursue in vain efforts to continue to look young? Has this perspective of the endless pursuit for the fountain of youth even infected and affected the way you look at the Bible, at Christianity, even at God? Take time now to evaluate your own assumptions about what counts as young and what counts as old and whether one is more important than the other, or not.

Sixteenth Sunday of the Year

The Christian's Obligation
6/21/77

"Who are You, Sir?" —Acts 9.5

The Christian commits himself totally and without reservation to Christ as Lord and Savior. We may ask who is this Christ who demands that I give my all to Him, to follow Him the rest of my life wholly and completely? Then we ask the question that Paul asked 2,000 years ago—"Who is this man with so much power, who is this Christ?"

We know he was a man who came and lived among the people. We know that He became hungry and thirsty as we do. We know that He had friends and yet sometimes He felt lonely. We know that He went to the tomb of a loved one. The Bible says He was tempted as we are, but He was also more than a man. He said, "Before Abraham was, I am." This set Him apart from every other person that ever lived. The glory of God is summed up in the incarnation, the coming of the Son of God to earth. God has taken up residence with humankind.

Paul declared that Jesus is the image of the invisible God, the first born of all creation. He is before all things, and in Him all things hold together. If He ever took His hand off the world it would explode into millions of pieces. It may seem impossible but that is what the Scriptures teach. He was fully man and also fully God. That's the mystery and the wonder of the incarnation. The Word became flesh and dwelled among us. He made the blind to see and the deaf to hear, the dumb to speak and He fed the hungry.

Then we are reminded of what John said: "The Word became flesh and lived among us." He has compassion upon us. He even knows the number of hairs on our heads. He sees the smallest bird that falls. On the cross He took upon Himself your sins and mine. His ministry only lasted three years, but what a ministry! He went to the tomb and on the third day He arose, and lives forever as King of kings and Lord of lords. Our salvation does not rest upon our works or our money but rather it depends on the grace of God. God is constantly working in us to will and to do His good pleasure. The question is—Are you following Him?

8/22/71

"Run your best race of faith and win everlasting life for yourself, for it was to this life you were called by God when you made your good confession of faith before many witnesses." —1 Timothy 6.12

Paul tells Timothy to look upon life as a continuous warfare against the evil forces in a tumultuous world. This advice to Timothy is also meant for us today. They are words of warning and of comfort. In these days of distrust and of lack of faith, of pain and misery, we should not spend our days as weak, ignorant, despondent, sorrowful people. We should live as human beings fulfilling our calling and be girded with the reality of faith in Christ Jesus, advanced in the knowledge that God is the merciful Protector, the giver of every good gift, who has overturned the power of darkness and has established His kingdom of righteousness and the sanctifying truth of His holy Word. If we receive it rightly it shall work in us a willingness to be obedient to His will and serve Him with seriousness and simplicity, deliberate trust and deep humility.

Christian life is a warfare. It needs an earnest spirit, and our fullest determination to obey God's voice. Self-confident people do not know their own hearts and do not fear God. They have no encouraging message amid the terrors and the threatenings of an evil world. But the Word of God which is the eternal truth, creates in us joy, courage, hope, devotion, fruitfulness and life, yes even everlasting life. If we strive with faith, with works of charity and love, we please God. He will bless and strengthen every feeble effort we make for a truly consecrated life.

Questions and Thoughts for Reflection

1. Perhaps the most important religious question ever asked is "how do you evaluate Jesus?" The answer to that question speaks volumes about your own faith and beliefs. If you think Jesus was just a remarkable human being, a teacher, a prophet, perhaps even a healer, and a good moral example, that belief doesn't require that you worship Him as King of kings and Lord of lords. That belief allows you to keep the one who says, "Behold I stand at the door and knock" at arms length and does not require of you some sort of ultimate commitment of your life. Indeed, you could believe that about the historical Jesus and it not change your life orientation much at all, other than admiring the man as a remarkable person. But when St. Paul asked, "Who are you, sir?" the answer was not merely shocking but deeply troubling—"I am Jesus who you have been persecuting." Have you ever had the experience of being so deeply wrong about something in life that it caused you to doubt your own sanity and self-confidence, and whole belief system? Paul had such an experience. Notice that Jesus doesn't say "Saul, Saul why are you persecuting my followers?" No, He asks, "Why are you persecuting ME?" But Jesus is revealing Himself as a heavenly being, someone dwelling in glory with God the Father. How could anyone be persecuting Him? That is until one realizes that "inasmuch as you have done it unto the least of these, you have done it unto me." Jesus is so spiritually united with and connected to His followers on earth, indeed He is "Christ in us the hope of glory," or as Paul himself would later say, "Christ lives in me," that an assault on His followers is an assault on Him personally.

The story of the U Turn on Damascus Road that led Saul the persecutor to become the apostle of Christ to the Gentiles raises disturbing questions for those who would trivialize Jesus as just another remarkable human being, questions like, Why do I not believe this story in Acts 9 is true? Why must I try to explain away the resurrection appearances of Jesus? Why am I so convinced that miracles can't happen despite all the evidence to the contrary? If you know someone like this, and they are a friend or family member, at some point you need to gently and in love ask them—Who do you say He is? Perhaps that will be that person's Damascus Road moment.

2. Recently we have been regaled with the horrors of the war in Ukraine and all the atrocities being committed there by the Russian forces. It is tempting to be thankful we don't live in that war zone and think we are safe where we are (despite continued hideous gun violence of all sorts killing hundreds of Americans because our politicians refuse to enact adequate gun control laws like those that exist in other more civilized countries, even though the majority of Americans support such laws). Paul however reminds Timothy and us that in fact we are in a war zone; we are in a spiritual war, wherever we live in the world, only many Christians are oblivious to this fact. Whatever you may think about guns as means of protection, for sure, they cannot protect you from the Devil or for that matter from yourself.

Paul in Ephesians 6 says our weapons of war against the powers of darkness are faith, hope, love, and other Christian virtues and of course the mighty Gospel. Sometimes Christians have mistakenly thought that Ephesians 6.10-20 is a call to go on the offensive against the powers of darkness, to deliberately choose to engage in spiritual warfare. In fact, it is not such a call. The repeated verb in this passage is *Stand*, and *Withstand*. The spiritual weapons Paul mentions are sufficient to protect us from the onslaught of evil, but they are defensive weapons. They do not come with a clarion call to "charge the enemy." How have you evaluated passages like 1 Timothy 6.12 or Ephesians 6.10-20? What sort of posture do you take about spiritual warfare? Have you ever read C. S. Lewis's classic book *The Screwtape Letters* in which the Devil says to his demons, "the best trick we have to deceive the believer is to convince them we do not exist"? Think about these things.

Seventeenth Sunday of the Year

Soul Food
6/19/79

Our souls are a mirror, a reflection of the divine. There is a divine spark in every one of us. That's why we dream and sing and hope and laugh and feel for others. That's why we pray and link ourselves to the Creator of the world. That's why heroes give up their lives for other people and human beings continue to evolve from being primitive to a superior state of civilized human being. It also accounts for love, conscience, and a craving for peace despite all wars.

He who feels the presence of God within himself is blessed with a tremendous power to achieve the impossible. Every time we move a spade or rake the ground and plant a seed we are imitating our Creator. The first gardener was God. "And the Lord God planted a garden in Eden, and everything pleasant and good grew and became beautiful." It would be hard to count the many miracles. The perfections of all living things happen with the rotation of the seasons. The spring, the summer, the fall and the winter all bring beauty. God touches all these with His fingers and they take on garments of color and glory and beauty.

A touch of mysticism is good for the soul. It makes life richer and more meaningful. All of the great religious founders were mystics. They felt the presence of God in their lives. Some even claimed to hear His voice. It is sometimes difficult to understand what goes on in other people's minds. Silence or sometimes a facial expression can tell us more than words. The most precious vocabulary is the language of the heart.

The sages of old said, "be deliberate in judgment." They knew the dangers of stupid decisions and immoral and amoral ways. What we do and say can affect many people. So then let us be deliberate in our judgment, and weigh all sides of every question so as not to hurt another person, relying on the Holy Spirit for guidance. Let us treat our fellow human beings as we would like them to treat us, letting the Holy Spirit guide us on the way to eternal glory.

What Way Are We Traveling?
11/13/77

"In the beginning God . . . ." These words are the cornerstone of all existence. Without God there would have been no beginning. Millions of people worship many things instead of worshipping this Creator God. They find no answers to life's difficulties and are frustrated. Just as Adam was made for fellowship with God, so are all people. Jesus said, "You shall love the Lord your God with all your heart, and with all your soul, and with all your mind, and with all your strength, and love your neighbor as yourself."

As we seek God, what route do we take? How can a finite human being understand an infinite God? There are so many mysteries and miracles happening all around us each day that we do not understand even though they seem simple, yet we cannot explain them. Then what about the laws of nature and the universe? Who can explain reproduction? We read the Bible every day, year in and year out and yet there is so much of it that is too deep for us.

Jesus said, "there is a wide road to destruction, and a narrow road to heaven." The direction we go will determine whether or not we find ourselves and God. In this age our most important quest is our personal search for God and answers concerning life. If human beings could 'prove' God, then God would be no greater than us. Faith is the link between us and God. The Bible says you must believe He exists, and God gives us evidence, reasons to do so. God has taken it upon Himself to encourage our faith. God pursues us just as we are searching for Him. The way we travel makes the difference.

In spite of human rebellion, God loves us with an everlasting love. When human beings chose in the Garden of Eden to defy

God's law, they broke fellowship with God. Good and evil cannot live together. Which road are you traveling? John said "God is love." Are we seeking God's love or are we trying to be independent, to go our own way? Everlasting love and eternal bliss await us. God is seeking us every day. He never lets up for He loves us so much, He gave Himself as a ransom for us.

Questions and Thoughts for Reflection

1. There has been much talk in the Christian community, and numerous books written in recent years about creation care, about our human responsibility to take care of God's creation and not keep abusing it with pollution and other things that have brought about climate change. The ice caps are melting the oceans are rising, and wind and fire storms are raging far more often than in the past in places as diverse as California and Australia. I was recently doing a teaching module in Colorado Springs and my host took me to the west side of town where they were rapidly building 30,000 new condos. Why, I asked? The answer was that the exodus had begun from the portions of California burned to a crisp, and many of the movers were coming to Colorado Springs. But alas, Colorado Springs and indeed the population belt in Colorado are in trouble as well. There has been drought and the aquifers are drying up and when they are gone, they cannot be replenished—here comes the new desert in Colorado. Meanwhile the snowpack in the Alps is far below normal and that is the source of water for Switzerland and other countries. I do not want to be a prophet of doom, but all of this illustrates what a poor job we have done in following God's original instructions to Adam and Eve, namely tended the garden, plant the seeds, nurture and take care of the earth which feeds us.

There is a reason Paul warned us in Rom. 8 that all of creation is groaning, longing for its own renewal when the resurrection and the new creation dawns. So practically speaking what should we as Christians do about this problem? Well for one thing conservative Christians should be concerned enough to be conservationists of the good earth. My grandfather pointed out that all the great religious leaders were in one sense mystics, visionaries. They were hopeful about the future and they reminded us that without vision the people perish. What are you hopeful about these days? Do you care what happens to the earth, the air, the water, the eco-system we need to live and move and have our being?

2. At one point in Pop's second lesson for today he says, "If human beings could 'prove' God, then God would be no greater than us." This is worth pondering. Human knowledge, while it is ever increasing over time, is nonetheless always going to be finite. It is difficult enough for a finite being to conceive of and partially understand an infinite one, never mind be able to know that infinite one in the same way we may know, for instance, the laws of nature. And so I think my grandfather is right—we can provide evidence for the existence of God, but not some sort of airtight proof, though the philosophers among us have tried hard to do so. If God could be reduced to our level and our capacity to know, He wouldn't be God. This is why faith is so important, it is at best a sort of partial knowledge coupled with trust for the parts we cannot know or understand. What would you consider the strongest evidence for God's existence, and more importantly for the content that He loves us profoundly and has even come to dwell with us for a time in the person of Jesus?

Eighteenth Sunday of the Year

A Story to Tell to the Nations
3/25/79

The Gospel of Jesus Christ is Good News, the best news in the world. It is a love story to surpass all other love stories. It is definitely the news the world needs to hear. If you have this story, you have a duty to share it. Every Christian has obligated himself to go into all the world and tell the Good News to every creature. It is greater and stronger than anything a human being can imagine or dream up.

The story is a message to fallen human beings, it is about a birth in Bethlehem, agony in a garden, a trial before Pilate, a cross on Calvary. It is also a story about a thorn crowned brow, nail pierced hands, and a wounded side. It is a record of a tragic Friday afternoon, a gloomy Saturday, and a victorious Sunday morning. Christ really died while on that cross. Jesus said many things, but one of the bandits failed to get a word from Him, and yet the silence seemed to say "you just wait until Sunday morning." It seemed to say it's better to come out of the grave than to come down from the cross. Then Jesus dropped His head to His shoulder and died. But let's not dwell on that too long.

Let us hasten to say that He was laid in a borrowed tomb, but why a borrowed tomb? Because He would not be there permanently. He would only use it for two nights. Joseph must have known this, so Jesus only remained there until His resurrection. And according to the plan the angels rolled away the slab on Sunday morning, and Jesus came forth in all power in the orbit of the omnipotent. He stood on the Mt. of Olives and said, "Go into all the world and preach the Gospel to every creature." It is our duty to tell it to everybody everywhere until every land becomes a new Jerusalem and a house of prayer, until every sinner has been saved by grace. We all have this story to tell.

3/21/82

"We should not trust in ourselves but in God, who delivered us from so great a death, in whom, we trust, will yet deliver us." —2 Corinthians 1.9-10

The life of the apostle Paul is a life of superlatives. He excelled in zeal, in work, and in suffering. He was misunderstood, criticized and persecuted. He traveled extensively, and he accomplished great things for the Lord. His writings reflect the superb psychology of a life hid with Christ in God. Paul's life was superlative because he remembered the God of the past, observed the God of the present, and expected that same God to continue to deliver him. In this we find the tenses of a victorious and superlative life.

"Our memory brings to mind who delivered us from so great a death." The word "us" is significant. God has delivered us from death, but also from violence, despair, bereavement and disease. Even sin has not overcome us. We are yet alive in body, mind and in spirit. Truly the Lord has helped us and He will deliver. So, Paul observes that God is now delivering us. In Him we live and move and have our being. God delivers us from despair even in the valley of the shadow of death. God said my grace is sufficient for you. Let not your heart be troubled. What matters is the one in whom we trust, trusting that He will deliver us.

There is no question about it. This deliverance will come through Jesus Christ the Lord. So let our memory of the past added to the observation of the present prompt sincere and unwavering faith, in confident expectation of all the good God has in store for us. And this includes everlasting life in that beautiful land where there is no sin or sorrow, but eternal bliss forever—in that house not made with hands, eternal in the heavens. Amen

Questions and Thoughts for Reflection

1. There are all sorts of stories in the Bible, but the red thread that runs right through the Bible is the story of God's love for human beings and His efforts to redeem and restore fallen humanity. But, of course, you have to first know you are lost before you can realize that you need to be saved. Lots of people have no clue they need to be saved, indeed many of them think they are doing quite well on their own. There is a reason for the old saying "blessed are those who know their need for God." What exactly do you do with people who have no interest in, and have no sense that they need Christ in their lives? Sometimes there is nothing you can do at the cognitive level. You can pray for the person, even pray for some dramatic event in their lives to happen so they will realize their need for God. But sometimes you just have to set a good example, and be a silent witness to a better way of living out one's days.

One of the odder comments in all of these lessons is the suggestion that Joseph of Arimathea knew that Jesus was only using His tomb for a short period of time. What do you make of this suggestion? Yes, Jesus was buried in a borrowed tomb, which speaks volumes about the failures of His brothers who had a duty to provide a decent burial for Him. And yes, Jesus had anticipated His own resurrection "on the third day" after His death, and so a borrowed tomb would work fine. But Joseph? How could he have known this? Was it because as a person who had heard Jesus, a person who was seeking God's kingdom, he had heard Jesus say I'll be raised from the dead shortly after I die? It's perhaps possible but seems to read a lot into the story.

2. I have been saved, I am being saved, and I shall be saved. There are in fact three tenses to salvation in Paul's way of thinking, and initial salvation needs to be followed by sanctification and then final salvation at the resurrection of believers when they are conformed to the image of Christ, even in the body. My grandfather is right that Paul understood, even through his own personal experience of God, that God has a track record of having already delivered Him in part, which leads Him to have confidence about the deliverance yet to come. How about you? Do you realize that you are not yet fully

saved, sanctified and glorified, and the best is yet to come? Do you face the future with hope and confidence? The author of Hebrews says "faith is the assurance of things hoped for." Does that describe what you have in your heart and mind?

Nineteenth Sunday of the Year

The Glory of God
12/4/77

John tells us that God has declared His glory. He also reminds us that we have seen His glory. Many people in Jesus' day did not see the glory of God fully. Judas did not see the glory of God in Christ. Pilate didn't see it. The unrepentant bandit on the cross didn't see it. And there are many people today who do not see it. God has never promised believers an utopia. Jesus said you would have to enter by the narrow way if you follow Him. Yes, the way to everlasting life is hard, and those who find it are few.

God said if we would declare His glory, we must go and carry the Gospel to all nations. He said, "You shall be my witnesses in Jerusalem, in all of Judaea and Samaria and to the ends of the world." We must reach out to those around us. We may be here for a short time or a long time. No one knows. But there is a feeling that we better work while we can for the night is coming when no one can work. Jesus said, "If anyone would come after me let him deny himself, take up his cross and follow me."

Are you ready to do that? Are you ready to make His goals your first priority? It requires commitment. It involves the whole person—the intellect, the will, all of it. We must live out what we profess. He said we would be known by our fruit. The greatest fruit we can bear is love. Do we really love the world and its people for whom Christ died? Are we practicing that love? This way of living will be hard. Throughout history the totally committed Christians have been a suffering people, a persecuted people. Yes, it costs to follow Christ.

But if you have glimpsed the glory of what God has done for us, no price is too high to pay to declare His glory. Our salvation does not rest upon our works or our money. It is much deeper than that. Our salvation rests upon the grace of God. God's resources are available, but are you ready to accept them?

5/6/79

"Blessed are the poor in spirit for theirs is the Kingdom of Heaven."
—Matthew 5.3

Jesus found springs of happiness in areas of human experience which to other persons seemed forbidding and dry. Poverty is one such area. In connection with it He named seven others. He might have named many more but these are enough for His purposes.

Was He right? Can the poor be happy and blessed? Those who accept a commitment to the common good (see Acts 2 and 4) as the limit of their own economic hope and desire are the poor in spirit, for what one owns in this world is incidental, because ownership is really just stewardship of things for the common good, or else it is robbery.

Among the poor in spirit, the Kingdom of Heaven is a blessed reality—it is theirs. Such people as these are spiritually prepared to take a true view of life's values, to have access to the highest values and to appreciate them. Faith, hope, and love find in such a spirit a fertile soil and freedom of growth. This is especially true of Jesus, the homeless man. He is the sharer of poverty with them and also He shares with them His great enterprise of bringing in the Kingdom of God, in which that poverty which blights and curses the poor will no longer exist on earth, and beyond this life a heavenly home awaits them. Consider Lazarus in the parable of the rich man and Lazarus (Luke 16). Blessed indeed are the poor in spirit, for theirs is already the Kingdom of heaven.

Questions and Thoughts for Reflection

1. What exactly is glory, biblically speaking? On the one hand there are places in the Bible that suggest that the Hebrew word *kavoth*

refers to God's living presence or at least the effect of that presence. So, when the Gospel says "we have seen his glory" this means that the disciples have seen the living presence of God in Christ. There are other places in the Bible where "glory" seems to refer to what we as believers are to do—glorify God through our lives and perhaps especially by worshipping Him in spirit and in truth. There are still other places where we hear of God glorifying His own name, which seems to refer to His vindicating of His honor, and we also hear about Him glorifying His Son Jesus. There is, in short, a variety of ways this idea is used in the Bible.

What we should not think is that God is a glory grabber, one who jealously wants to be given all the credit for everything good and never gives glory to others. This clearly is not true—God glorifies His Son, and also His believers by placing His spirit, His living presence within us. Notice for instance in that great Christ hymn in Philippians 2.5-11 that God highly exalts Christ after His death on the cross, and gives Him the name which is above all names—which by the way is not the name Jesus, a name He already had, but rather the divine name, the name risen Lord, and indeed God. God is indeed a glory giver, and glory in any case is not a zero-sum game, as if the glorifying of Christ takes away from the glory of the Father, or the sanctifying and indwelling in the believer somehow subtracts something from God's glory and living presence. How have you thought about glory in the past? Did you understand the range of meaning of the term? Why do you think God desires to share His glory?

2. The second lesson for today is a challenging one for overly materialist American Christians who have believed the false Gospel of health and wealth. My grandfather rightly insists on the passages at the end of Acts 2 and Acts 4 as modeling how Christians should think about property—namely "the earth is the Lord's and the fullness thereof." We are not owners of anything. Rather we are stewards of God's property. He made all things, including all persons, and we all belong to Him. The Bible does not affirm either the notion of strictly private or strictly public property. It affirms that all property belongs to God, and we should be using it for His glory, for the

edification of human beings, and should cultivate a sense of detachment from our culture's insistence on our need to buy and buy and buy things, often things we don't even need.

This brings us to where that second lesson begins. Why do you think Jesus said "blessed are the poor in spirit," or even, if we follow the Lukan version of the saying, "blessed are the poor"? One writer has suggested that what the saying really means is blessed are those who know their need for God, and that definitely defines the poor, who cannot trust in or rely on their copious possessions because they don't have them! John Wesley preached a sermon to his Methodists titled "On the Use of Money" which had three points—make all you can by honest means, save all you can, and give all you can. He says if you only do the first or the first and the second you may be a living person but you are also a dead Christian. What do you think about that assertion? Have your possessions come to have such importance in your life that in a sense they have come to possess you, to dictate how you behave especially in regard to the protection of those possessions? Think on these things.

Twentieth Sunday of the Year

10/21/79

"Listen to me, you who pursue righteousness and who seek the LORD: Look to the rock from which you were cut and to the quarry from which you were hewn." —Isaiah 51.1

Many people in this country today assert that their heritage is not very important. Some say that relationships with those of the past are a thing of the past. This is terrible mistake. How can one interpret the present and courageously and intelligently face the future if he doesn't know or remember or honor the past? Centuries ago, the prophet Isaiah echoed a similar call to Israel declaring "look to the rock from which you were hewn." In other words, you need to know where you have come from in order to know where you are going.

We should be proud of our positive heritage and carefully reflect on the rock from which we were hewn. The book of Joshua is the kind of book from which any man or woman can receive inspiration every day. The beginning of the book basically divides things into three thoughts. The first is that God speaks to Joshua. The second is that Joshua tells the people exactly what God said. And the third is that the people do exactly what God wants them to do.

In the fourth chapter an interesting scene takes place when the whole nation had crossed the Jordan and the Lord said to Joshua, "Choose twelve men, one from each tribe and command them to take twelve stones from the middle of the Jordan from the very place where the priests were standing. Tell them to carry the stones with them and put them down where they would camp tonight, one for each of the tribes of Israel. These stones will remind the people of what the Lord has done." Somehow, we can see these twelve men going out into the riverbed, the water had been parted and held on either side, with each one carrying as big a stone as he could carry to shore.

Then as God tells us they went back and gathered twelve more stones. God then told them, "I want one monument built in the middle of the river, and the other one built on the shore." This was a strange request for God to make. But neither Joshua nor the men questioned it at all. The stones in the river tell us one fact and those on the shore tell us another. Those in the river say in time of drought or times of flood (i.e., in times of trouble) whatever the problems of life may be, God was with you. The stones on the bank symbolize another fact. They say this is the beginning, but there is no question as to what the future holds. It holds victory.

These stones point to a time when God's people co-operated with Him. Our own nation has been brought together so that we might do well for God, home, and country. We should become cornerstones looking well to our heritage and to prepare for the future. Let us look over our shoulders at our personal pilgrimage. Let us look at the crises that wash upon our own personal shores, our churches, our homes, our communities. These are all built on rocks from the past. Let us look well to the rock from which we were hewn. Although the stones are worn smooth by the turbulence of humankind, let them be strong and reveal a monument to victory. Victory for God, home, and country. That should be the goal of every human being. Always remember that everything you do or say, large or small, good or bad becomes a part of your life for as long as you live.

1/18/79

"Remember what happened long ago. Acknowledge that I am God and that there is none other like me. From the beginning I told you what would happen." —Isaiah 46.9

In saying this, Isaiah didn't mean for us to brood on past things but to use them to go forward. Our inspiration is from the past. We recognize however that our duty is in the present. So be it. But we are also aware that our future is now. Without actions based on good purposes we can slide into oblivion as a nation whose people failed, for whatever reasons, to recognize and do their duty, both political and religious duty.

It is the irrefutable truth that each generation of people must earn the right to be free. What can we as Christians do to protect our way of life, not only from our enemies in war but also protect from the imbalance in our society stemming from greed and the consumption of raw materials of the earth at the expense of the balance of nature.

The changing moral habits of our people have contributed to the current low level of morality. We can remember when families attended the movies that were not pornographic. We remember when public opinion was so great that aspirin was about the only drug you could get without a prescription. The powerful forces of selfishness and greed are responsible for the present dilemma. Desecration of our flag, use of drugs, and leniency of the courts in capital crimes all characterize our country now. Also, there are the white-collar criminals who continue to steal from businesses and we as consumers pay for it.

We are bombarded every day by television, radio, the press, periodicals with evidence that our moral condition is getting worse day by day. The time to do something about it is now. The place to start is in the U.S.A. If our great republic is to survive as a beacon for all people everywhere we must turn to the past for guidance and inspiration. We must act in the present with hope for the future. The Lord said, "Whom shall I send and who will go for me?" What is your answer?

Questions and Thoughts for Reflection

1. Historical amnesia is a dangerous disease. As has been said those who forget the past are bound to repeat its mistakes. The past is important both positively and negatively. Negatively we must learn from the mistakes of the past. Positively, we must appreciate and remember and honor the good heritage we have as Christians. Isaiah's exhortation was calling his people in or just beyond exile to remember

the distant past, remember Abraham and Sarah, for example and all they went through in a life which involved trusting God, and sometimes failing to do so as well. There has been a recent surge of interest because of website like Ancestry.com in our own ancestors. And there is nothing wrong with exploring that sort of heritage. But more important than tracing our lineal ancestors is learning from our Christian ancestors. And of course, sometimes the persons in question are both—both physical and spiritual ancestors who have much to teach us. One such ancestor for me who has served both roles is my grandfather. Take some time today to think through who your spiritual ancestors are and what you may owe to their influence in one way or another. Thank God for them, and ask yourself what new lessons you may still glean from their example and their legacy.

2. Our second lesson for today has a somewhat similar theme as the first. But here we learn that we cannot dwell in the past, but must learn from it. We must know and acknowledge our past but not make the mistake of facing backwards and living in that past. Yet many churches make this mistake. It has been said that the words that could be written over the front door of many churches is "We've Never Done It Like That Before." There is even a caricature of a famous hymn that goes like this "Like a mighty turtle moves the church of God/ Brothers we are treading where we've always trod/ Not united brethren, not one body we/ We shall all be standing here until eternity/ Backward Christian soldiers . . . ." Sadly, this does describe many churches today.

My grandfather also suggests that one of the reasons for the decline in the morality of our nation in the last many decades is precisely because we have forgotten our past, our heritage, not least of which includes the moral fiber of many of our Christian ancestors. They would have probably passed out if they realized that America would come to celebrate in the twenty-first century numerous forms of sexual immorality and then we wonder why there are so many sexually transmitted diseases plaguing our younger people. The church has not responded in any adequate way to these challenges. Perhaps God is asking again, as He asked Isaiah, "Who will go for me, and who will tell my stubborn people that they must change their ways?" Before we can hope to redeem our culture, we must first redeem our churches. Would you agree?

Mark Twain was a remarkable writer, and one of his more endearing traits was his honesty about his life and heritage. He tells the story of how he paid someone $50, a lot of money in the nineteenth century, to research his ancestry. And then with a pause he adds "and a $100 to cover it back up!" Sometimes what we learn about our past and our ancestors provides the lesson—"go and do otherwise." It's not always a lesson that implies "go and do likewise."

Twenty-first Sunday of the Year

Pentecost
4/1/79

"Jesus took bread and broke it and gave it to his disciples saying . . ." —Matthew 26:26

Why do we call communion the Lord's Supper? Not because Jesus kept it for Himself, but through His love He gave it to us. This is the paradox—that the only things we can claim are those we give away. Jesus was not a getter but a giver. He would not feed Himself in the wilderness of temptation even though He was famished, but in another wilderness He fed a multitude. He would not seek publicity by leaping from the temple pinnacle but He turned the spotlight on the widow's mite. He would not accept a material kingship but He set up a spiritual kingdom in which all are kings. Jesus said, "He that loses his life for my sake shall find it." He also said, "I lay down my life" and He matched His words with His deeds. His birth changed the course of world history. Human life became sacred and so did human birth. Motherhood ever since has been on a higher level. Even common bread when touched by Jesus was different.

At the last supper He took the bread and the cup and gave it to His disciples. Christians have always felt that here He gave more than taste or reason can discern. The most remarkable thing that happened is Jesus not only taught it but believed it, and practiced it. He still gives of Himself through word and sacrament so that He becomes ours and we become his. He said "my peace I give to you," and yet He is the Prince of Peace.

If the logic of all this seems confusing, the truth is that if we are not to lose our very souls we must give up our grasping greedy nature and replace it with a generous loving spirit, for living in Christ is giving. He is the bread of life. Christ can touch any ordinary life and make it significant and beautiful for it will reflect the light that shines in Him. His touch still has its ancient power and He is love, and He demands love, our love. He also demands we love one another as He loved us for to do this is like Christ. So, whenever we partake of the bread and the cup let us remember His words—"do this in remembrance of me." It represents His broken body on the cross for our sins. Has He touched your life? Does His light shine in you?

5/31/81

"And when the Day of Pentecost had come, they were all with one accord in one place." —Acts 2.1

Pentecost is the birthday of the church. Something monumental happened that day. We ask—what was it? Clearly, it was wonderful and miraculous. Luke attempts to describe the event. People no doubt asked him what happened. He said it was like a wind and it had the power of a cyclone. Then he said it was like a fire that burned all the sin away. It is as if tongues took all the embarrassed silence away and each person found himself speaking to His fellows at Pentecost, Matthew in Hebrew to a Hebrew speaker, Philip to a Greek, Joseph of Arimathea to the very rich, until each person finally heard them speaking in their own varied languages and understood it. It was like a divine intoxication that took away reserve and let them speak freely.

Luke has done the best he could for us, within the limits of human language, to tell us the story of what happened. But what did it accomplish? I can hardly explain except that each of the one hundred and twenty disciples arose from their knees and went out of the room and by three o'clock they were all back with each bringing about twenty-five of their own language or social group or class until when the last one came in, there were 3,000 present!

When Peter stood up to preach one suspects for sure he must have been very pleased. The stage was set for him to do a great work for Christ, when he gave the invitation to accept a crucified Christ, every one of those hands went up. The one hundred and twenty had done their personal work beforehand. We desperately need a Pentecost throughout the world today more than ever in our history. God grant that it may come again as there is too much apathy. We need it to start with us, in our church. Here and now.

Questions and Thoughts for Reflection

1. Christians over the ages have taken various different approaches, with different interpretations of the last supper and the Lord's Supper. What has too seldom been contemplated is the notion that Jesus was so sure of the outcome of His death that He believed He could symbolically give His disciples the benefits of that death *in advance* saying "this is my body broken for you," "this is my blood shed for you." Not only so, but He believed that His coming death would inaugurate the new covenant. When you think about it, this is simply astounding. Apparently, Jesus really did know in advance that His life would not end in death, that there would be a sequel without equal, namely His resurrection long before the general resurrection. If all this is true, that should certainly change how we view the Lord's Supper in which we remember and celebrate what Christ has done for us. The question we must ask ourselves is this—what exactly does the death of Jesus accomplish for us now, today, through the partaking of the Lord's Supper?

It seems very clear from 1 Corinthians 11.17-34 that Paul believes something more than pure symbols are involved in the Lord's Supper. He thinks there is some sort of spiritual transaction that happens, such that if someone partakes of the Lord's Supper in an unworthy manner, some sort of judgment falls upon that person. The contrary of that would be that if one participates in a worthy manner, some sort of blessing happens. The simplest way to explain the latter is that Jesus is spiritually present with the Eucharist when you are partaking of it, and so it is Jesus Himself whom you are encountering in that act. It is a high and holy moment.

Notice as well that Paul reminds us that the Lord's Supper is for every believer, and that it is supposed to bring us together with each other as well as uniting us with Christ. Divisions and dissensions are completely inappropriate at the Lord's Table. They must be put aside. How have you viewed the Lord's Supper in the past? When I was pastoring many years ago, I had church members who knew that partaking of the Lord's Supper involved a spiritual moment and transaction, and they refrained from doing so, because they felt unworthy. But this ceremony is not about us *being* worthy, it is about partaking in an worthy manner. None of us are worthy of what Christ did for us on the cross! This is why most rituals of the Lord's Supper include a confession of sins before we partake—"we confess we have sinned"—and then the minister says, "in the name of Jesus Christ you are forgiven." Do you understand that the Lord's Supper is about union and communion with the Holy One and that that is only possible if our sins are and have been forgiven? Think on these things.

2. Pentecost, in many Protestant churches is often a day when one thinks about the Great Commission to share the Gospel with the world. But we should remember in the first place that it was about empowerment for that mission. It was the day Joel's prophecy about all God's people being filled with the Holy Spirit became true and empowered the disciples for witness. In short it was about a miracle. But what was the miracle that happened? It was not just divine empowerment, it was also about inaugurating the mission at that Jewish festival by the Gospel being miraculously spoken in numerous different human languages so that the audience could exclaim "We heard them speaking in our own native tongues." This event was not about what came to be called glossolalia, the spiritual gift of speaking in an angelic prayer language to God. It was instead about a unique event of speaking in a foreign language one did not yet know. My Greek students keep praying it will happen again, that suddenly they will know and speak Greek, but alas, Pentecost like Jesus' death and resurrection was a unique and unrepeated miraculous event. Sometimes Pentecost has been called the reversal of what happen at the tower of Babel. But Pentecost doesn't change all the languages back

into one language, rather it makes clear the one Gospel can and should be spoken in all human languages.

How have you viewed Pentecost in the past? Do you realize that it suggests not only a worldwide mission beginning from Jerusalem, but it also suggests that the Gospel should be and can be indigenized in every language group and culture? The Gospel is the only message that can truly change anyone from any culture and this is why we have Bible societies who are still working hard to translate the Good News into the myriad of human languages. Last time I checked there are still some 500 languages or dialects which have no words of the Gospel yet translated into their tongues, but the American Bible Society, and Wycliffe and many others are working on it. And we as the church should be generously supporting such work. Does your church have this important task in their budget?

Twenty-second Sunday of the Year

7/22/79

"And if I go and prepare a place for you, I will come back and take you to be with me that you also may be where I am." —John 14.3

It is essential for human beings to have a home, a place to live, to shelter from the elements, a place to go to be comfortable and feel safe. The Bible and history itself tell us of this fundamental aspect of our nature. According to research the first homes were caves. Even in such a place we wished to decorate, for archaeological sites reveal crude drawings on cave walls. In addition, early humans provided their homes with compartments to store food and wood for a fire. Today we are basically doing the same thing, following the same patterns. How far have we actually come from the cave dweller? Now we look for a location, build our homes hoping for quality in the homes we build for we want it to last, and we want it to be comfortable, a place where we can have peace. We make agonizing mortgage payments, pay irritating light and water bills, and terrible tax payments. And yet, in spite of all this we are pleased with ourselves for we have done what every decent person should do, provide for himself, for his family, for his loved ones.

God must be pleased for humans to have these basic material things but God didn't intend for us to have just one home. He wanted us to have a material home and also a spiritual home. While the material home is pretty comfortable and convenient, the spiritual home must be more beautiful, comfortable and convenient. When you start the construction of your spiritual home and follow the plan

God has drawn up for you, not only can you live in your pleasant material house, but also in a more beautiful one designed by the One we have acknowledged as the Supreme Being. In this subdivision of His creation there is no disagreeable weather, no decay, no destruction by insects, and no mortgage payments, utility bills, or taxes. The plan of your heavenly home has already been drawn and prepared for by Jesus Himself. A picture of it has been painted by His Holy Word. To have the right and title to live in His subdivision is to acknowledge Him, trust Him, obey His commandments and do unto others as you would have them do unto you. You should study the teachings and plans of the supreme architect as outlined in John and elsewhere. And then, at the right time you will be allowed to move in, and He will provide all you need.

1/30/72

"Acquaint now yourself with Him, and be at peace. Thereby, good shall come unto you." —Job 22.21

A sense of the reality of God is the world's greatest need. The world is crying out for peace and prosperity, and our text here is the answer to this cry. Throughout all ages God has been trying to make Himself known to the human race. He sent judges, prophets, apostles and finally Christ, His only Son, to reveal Himself. Philip said, "Lord, show us the Father and it will suffice us," and Jesus replied, "He that has seen me, has seen the Father." Therefore, a father is the character or role in which God wants us to think of Him.

Another, though earthly, father, when his wayward son, poor and needy had turned his feet homeward, was seen by that father when he was a great way off. The father ran to meet him. Why was he in such haste? Not just because his own heart was yearning for his son. He was human. He hadn't been happy since his son had left home and he could not be happy without him. "Oh Ephraim, how can I give you up"—this is the cry of the father's heart, the human heart.

This is the source of our security, not just because of the fact that we love God, but that He loves us first, and not just because we hold His hand, but rather that He holds our hand and we feel and are secure in His hands. And we know He is able to keep us from falling and will one day present us faultless before the throne of Christ. Because of this I am convinced that He is able to keep that which I have committed to Him against that Day.

God says, "Fear not, for I am with you. Be not dismayed for I am your God. I will strengthen you and will help you and uphold you with the right hand of my righteousness. 'Thou art mine', sayeth the Lord."

Questions and Thoughts for Reflection

1. For many Christians ever since at least the Middle Ages, there has been an assumption that heaven is our final destination. This is understandable since Christ has not returned in 2,000 years, and increasingly the orientation of the church has become other-worldly when it comes to thinking about the endgame. And to be honest, the Gospel of John talks about Jesus going to prepare a place for us, apparently in heaven, because "in my Father's house there are many rooms." This other worldly home is what my grandfather is talking about, but notice that he says we are preparing for it, or even building it now. There has been a lot of Christian imaginative thinking about the heavenly home over the centuries. Some people talk about meeting their spouses or relatives in the 'sweet bye and bye' even though the Bible says nothing about physical family reunions in heaven. Indeed, only about 5% of the afterlife talk in the New Testament is about dying and going to heaven, whereas 95% is about the second coming of Christ to earth, the resurrection of the dead on earth, the last judgment on earth, and then the new heaven and new earth with God coming to dwell with us here. Even the most spiritual and visionary of all books, Revelation ends with a reunion with God here on earth—there is corporate merger of heaven and earth with the kingdom coming on earth as it has been in heaven.

The problem with simply focusing on heaven is that often the church has become too heavenly minded to be any earthly good. By this I mean that we have assumed that since we are leaving this world at death, that the mundane things of this world, including all its trials and tribulations are trivialized or made to seem of no great importance. "This world is not my home," said Larry Norman, "I'm just passing through." Now the problem with this is that the Bible insists God is the Creator God. He is not interested in exchanging His whole creation in exchange for some souls in heaven. He wants the renewal of His whole creation and His creatures.

Did you notice that the saint in heaven are singing the blues. The ones under the altar are asking, "How long, O Lord?" and they are given choir robes and told to hush (Rev 6.9-11). The point is, they are not satisfied with the lack of justice being done on earth, and the story of the Bible is in part that God will finally see justice done on earth, kingdom come on earth, God dwelling with His people on earth. This means that heaven is not our final destination or home. It's just an ultra-clean and nice B&B until the eschaton when Christ returns to earth *with* His saints. Ask yourself this question: if all this is true and is what the Bible teaches, how should this change my outlook about the importance of what we do here on earth? Indeed, on the importance of earth itself and our care for it. In what sense is heaven a home for those who die in Christ? And, if Christ is returning to dwell with us on earth, shouldn't we care how earth is and looks when He returns, so He will say, "I like what you've done with this place"?

2. The chief reason as Christians we image God as our heavenly Father is because Christ did so and He taught us to pray to God as Father. For Jesus, God was quite literally His Father, as He was the only begotten Son. We do not call God Father because the first person of the Trinity is a male for as Jesus Himself reminds us, God is spirit. It is simply Jesus' human nature that is male, but that says nothing about the divine nature or essence of God.

One of the most poignant images of God Jesus leaves us with is in the parable of the prodigal son. Rembrandt's famous painting of this parable is poignant. It shows the father gently placing his large hands on the shoulders of his son as he kneels before him. But even before that, it depicts the father as eagerly running out to meet his returning prodigal. God is one who seeks and saves the lost, or as the famous poem says, God is the hound of heaven, pursuing us who continue to run away. C. S. Lewis tells of the day in Oxford at his college Magdalen College in which in essence God backed Lewis into a corner until his gave in to God and accepted him. He says of that day, "on that day I was the most reluctant convert in all of Christendom." This hardly sounds like the usual euphoric accounts of conversion. But in the end, it is comforting to know that God doesn't want to let any of His human beings be lost forever, so much so that He keeps pursuing us. The lesson in all this is clear: if God is not giving up on anyone, even the most prodigal of offspring, neither should we. Are we His emissaries seeking to save the lost? Have we tired of praying in our prayers for particular people to come to the Lord? Can we redouble our prayers and efforts?

Twenty-third Sunday of the Year

3/21/1971

"I have been crucified with Christ, and it is no longer I who live but Christ who lives in me." —Galatians 2.20

The world needs a fresh, living portrait of Jesus Christ. His noblest portrait is a transformed personality with God's divine love gleaming through it. Paul declared, "For me to live is for Christ to live again in me." Matthew portrays Him as a King, Mark reveals Him as a servant, Luke sets Him forth as the Son of Man, while John describes Him as the Son of God. While these are all true, they cannot adequately present the complete picture. The portrait which the world covets is to be found in a redeemed and consecrated life. Christians whose lives have been so marked by such deep spirituality have always maintained the supremacy of Jesus Christ.

Just before William Carey passed into fuller life, a friend happened to speak to him about his great work in India, but the humble missionary of the cross made reply, "when I am gone, talk not of Carey, talk of Carey's Christ." By our thoughts and lives we become like that to which we constantly look and about which we think. Look at sin long enough and its cruel lines of uncharitableness will soon be graven upon our faces. Behold the Lamb of God, which takes away the sin of the world and all His wonderful passion and purity will refine our natures, until the beauty of His holiness is seen in our lives. The world asks for a fresh portrait of Jesus, and where will they find that portrait? They will find it in the lives of Christians. Will the world see that portrait in you?

1/19/72

"Go sell all you have, give to the poor, and you will have riches in heaven, then come follow me." —Luke 18

A young ruler was still not satisfied, although he was very rich. He went to Jesus and said, "Good teacher, what can I do to inherit everlasting life?" Jesus asked him if he knew the commandments—do not murder, do not steal, do not lie, honor your father and mother. The young man replied, "Ever since I was very young, I have obeyed all the commandments." Jesus said, "You need to do one thing more—go sell all you have and give money to the poor, and then come follow me and I will give you riches in heaven." But when Jesus said this, the young man hung his head as this made him very sad, for he was very rich. He worshipped his money, he valued it above God's promise, how true this is for too many people today. They take God for granted.

The greatest challenge for this day and time is expressed in a simple question—will we take our Christian faith seriously? If our answer is yes, we must put our faith into action, on a personal, social, and national level. Can we accumulate while there are those who die of hunger and be satisfied with ourselves? Does any nation or people have a right to make decisions that will affect adversely other people of the world? Christ is requiring of us an honest and courageous examination of our own type of Christianity. He Himself said, "If anyone would come after me, let him take up his cross and follow me." Only a courageous and authentic Christianity can offer itself to the world as the answer of God to its problems. If we would follow Christ, we must so live, that His life and will, will be reflected in our daily life. True Christian stewardship comes to us through faith and love.

The Corinthians set aside their offering regularly, they gave according as God had prospered them. If we the members of Temple Baptist Church are the church, then why shouldn't we accept our responsibility to make our church go forward by each member having a fair share in the support, so that others might know of Christ. The second commandment says love thy neighbor as thyself. I know that each Christian rejoices in His heart to feel that he has at least a small part in spreading the Gospel and in winning lost people to Christ. Christ gave all for us, even life itself, He gave us all we have and all we are. Then why should we hesitate to give a portion of our earnings, our time and talents to carry His program to a lost world? Love of others is the key to heaven but faith unlocks the doors. Do you have the right key of faith? Are we good stewards for Christ?

Questions and Thoughts for Reflection

1. Our first lesson for today reminds me of the story of the medical missionary Dr. Fred Douglas Shepard who in the early twentieth century ministered to people of all religions. He especially helped the Armenians during the time of the Ottoman massacres in eastern Turkey. The story is told of how a small Muslim man was brought to his clinic in Aintab very ill indeed. And Dr. Shepard nursed him back to health but he also shared the Gospel. The Muslim man accepted Christ and returned to his village talking again and again about Jesus and Dr. Shepard. The local mullah or Muslim cleric came to the little man and said, "Why all this talk about Jesus? He was a prophet who died many centuries ago and you have never seen him." The little man responded, "No, I've not seen him in person, but I have seen Dr. Shepard and Christ lives in him." The question for us is, when people look at us and our lives, do they get a glimpse of Christ? It has been said that if we wish to win some for Christ, we ourselves must be winsome, Christlike in character. Does that describe you? Would those who know you best describe you in that way?

2. What people do with their money tells us a lot about not only their desires but also their character. The story of the pious young man who had been obedient to the Mosaic Law but knew something was still lacking in his life is a sad tale. And it could be retold of many wealthy pious people ever since then. One thing you can be sure of—whatever there is in your life that has usurped the place of God, and has become a golden calf for you, God will require it of you at some juncture. When Jesus says take up your cross and follow me, He is not talking about making small sacrifices in life to be a

follower of Christ. He is talking about laying everything we have and all that we are on the altar and sincerely asking God what would you have me do? What would you have me be? Have you ever had such a moment of commitment in your life? Notice that the pious young man is already a follower of the Biblical God. That is not the issue here. The issue is what he is willing to give and give up, as "the one thing lacking" to really become a follower of Christ and His example. What is that one thing lacking in your life?

In my home church in Charlotte, North Carolina, my father was a team captain on one of the stewardship teams who in the Fall would visit every church member in their homes and get their pledge cards indicating their level of support for the church in the coming year. On that team was a bright and successful young lawyer who wore Brooks Brothers suits and drove a fancy car. Financially he was doing just fine. On his visitation list was an elderly lady, basically a shut in who lived in a trailer on the edge of town, and lived on a fixed income. When the lawyer got to her house and saw the gravel driveway, the concrete steps leading up to an old and battered trailer, he resolved he would not ask the little old lady for money, but would have a nice chat with her and he himself would give some to the church on her behalf. They indeed had a nice chat over sweet tea and tollhouse cookies, and when the lawyer stood up to leave the lady said, "What just a minute, I have my pledge card on the refrigerator." The lawyer replied, "That's alright, ma'am, I realize you are on a fixed income, Social Security check I imagine, and I'll put in some extra on your behalf." Before he could even finish his sentence, she was in his face, and grabbed his lapels and pointed her little finger at him and said, "Don't you take away from me the privilege of giving to the cause of Christ. I know it's not much, but I want to give." Profoundly embarrassed and red in the face, the lawyer apologized, took her pledge card and quietly slipped out the door. My grandfather was right to exhort us all to give until it helps our church, and that every little bit counts. Is your church known for that kind of spirit and generosity?

Twenty-fourth Sunday of the Year

10/13/74

"For if someone with a weak conscience sees you, with all your knowledge, eating in an idol's temple will he not be emboldened to eat what is sacrificed to idols?" —1 Corinthians 8.10

What is the conscience? That little shock of reality which reminds us of what is right and what is wrong. Esau sold his birthright with profane indifference, yet what would he have given years later to have been able to change his father's mind. What bitter tears a few minutes of pleasure cost him.

Ahab said to Elijah when his royal chariot was accosted, "Have you found me, oh my enemy?" Why should he say this when a short time before they had parted as friends? The very spot where they met provides the answer. It was the vineyard of Naboth, which Ahab had obtained by murder. Now, because his conscience was troubling him, he called Elijah an enemy. Judas Iscariot, in the moment of his success, knew bitterest remorse. He wept and tried to give back the money he had been paid to betray Jesus, then he went out and hanged himself.

Felix the Roman governor stood trembling before the prisoner Paul in the Imperial Palace in Caesarea, because Felix was a slave of a guilty conscience. So then, what is conscience?

In Romans 2.15, Paul describes persons who show the work of the Law written in their hearts, their conscience also bearing witness, and their thoughts in the meanwhile accusing or excusing one another. God has put within each of us something that cries aloud against us whenever we do that which we know to be wrong. Conscience is the detective that watches the direction of our steps and decries every conscious transgression. Conscience is a vigilant eye before which each imagination, thought, and act is held up for either censure or approval.

A man once said conscience is a little three-cornered thing inside me. When I do wrong it turns around and hurts me very much, but if I keep on doing wrong it turns so much that the corners wear off and it doesn't hurt me anymore, and that is true of all of us. Conscience is the detective that stalks our steps, but can also be the voice of God, yes that little light of the soul.

10/8/72
"Be ye perfect as I am perfect." —Matthew 5.48

It is good for us from time to time to realize our nothingness, our incompleteness, and our deficiencies. We are apt to grow self-complacent, to thank God we are not as others are, but far better. This feeling arises from the low standards we set before us. We compare ourselves with one another, with those around us, and in doing so we are not wise. Now in Matthew 5.48 we have startling words. This is a startling command, and it is a command which many of us simply pass over and ignore as impracticable and impossible.

Perfect, we say, perfect as God is perfect? Impossible! Imperfection marks everything and must mark everything here below. It is romantically idealistic to expect to attain that which is plainly out of our reach. And so, without further deliberation we quietly ignore the words altogether and to the vast majority of Christians they are a dead letter . . . and yet spoken by our Lord. They must surely have some plain and implied meaning. They tell us plainly what our aim must be. In this life we may never reach it. True to the very end, we shall fall far below it. But it will not do to have a lower standard than this. We must be ever striving to lift ourselves up to it more and more, and then more and more our life will be perfected here, until at last we come by His almighty power "unto a perfect man, unto to the measure of the stature of the fullness of Christ." So, we must always be striving for perfection, while knowing we cannot attain it in this life.

Questions and Thoughts for Reflection

1. Paul is not a person who coined the phrase "let your conscience be your guide," not least because as our first lesson for today suggests, the conscience can be anesthetized by repeated sin. It may shock us that there are people in this world who can coldly kill other human beings for no good reason and sleep very well at night. Their conscience doesn't bother them in the least. Nevertheless, Paul has some important things to say about conscience as a supplement of sorts to the guidance of God's Word. He talks about people with weak consciences in 1 Corinthians 8–12. Interestingly he is talking about people who have too many scruples about food, about what they eat. He is not talking about people who have too few scruples as we might expect. He refers to such hyper-sensitive persons as having a weak conscience. The lesson he draws leads to the conclusion that those with stronger consciences who don't have too many scruples about food, should not violate the weaker brothers or sisters by insisting they eat certain things. That's unloving.

Paul agrees with the strong about food issues, but defends the ones with the weak conscience. The real bottom line here is whatever a particular Christian cannot do in good faith, they should not do, because doing it will be a sin for them—a violation of their conscience. One more point: Paul is discussing what we would call adiaphora, things indifferent, things about which there are no specific commandments for Christians—for example what we should wear, what we should eat, what sort of cars we should drive etc.? In fact, most of the decisions we make day to day involve things that the Bible doesn't mention. In such circumstances, this passage in 1 Corinthians gives guidance. Some Christians have scruples about drinking wine or any alcoholic beverage, some do not. Whatever we do about such issues (and yes wine in Jesus' day involved alcohol, though it was not usually a high percentage of alcohol as they tended to water it down) we must do it only in good faith. We should never ever in any case harm our fellow believers who have many scruples by trying to get them to share our own belief and practices about such matters. Would you agree? What things that the Bible does not discuss do you have issues of conscience about?

2. The concept of perfection, and even the term itself conjures up images of something a human being could never achieve, not least because we are all flawed human beings. But the passage in question is not dealing with perfection in the abstract. It is talking about being loving like the heavenly Father is loving, being perfected in love, not having perfect thoughts. In fact, since Jesus was teaching His disciples in Aramaic He was likely talking about being content with God's providing us with the basic necessities of life, and being generous with others who are in need. He was not talking about having some sort of spiritual experience called perfection. The context of the passage makes this rather clear. If we are to be perfect or complete as the heavenly Father is, remember the heavenly Father didn't need to have some spiritual experience of perfection. What we need is the love of God so poured into our hearts and lives that we will behave in the same compassionate way God does to us. What have been your most profound experiences of God's love? How have they motivated you to be more Christ-like in behavior?

Twenty-fifth Sunday of the Year

10/27/68

"But you shall receive power from on high . . . and you shall be my witnesses . . ." —Acts 1.8

Many church members have never been born again. The greatest need of the church is Spirit-born, Holy Ghost baptized Christians. When a church member loves the same kind of life that the godless worldly men or women do, he can be sure that he has never received the baptism of the Holy Spirit. The Holy Spirit is a divine personality, just as real as Jesus Christ or God the Father. The baptism of the Spirit has been promised to every Christian. The Scripture commands every Christian to be filled with the Holy Spirit. If you are to receive the Holy Spirit, there must be a real desire and longing in your heart for Him. Your heart and life must be clean and made ready for Him. You must give up every known sin and make full surrender to Christ.

The Christian that has been baptized with the Holy Ghost will witness for Christ with boldness and assurance. He will speak with an increasing knowledge of God's word and His power to save. He will not fulfill the lusts of the flesh. He will not be conformed to this world. He will live for Christ. He will manifest the fruit of the Spirit, which is love, joy, peace, long-suffering, kindness, goodness, faithfulness, meekness, and self-control. He will walk by the Spirit. He will manifest a gift of the Spirit. His life will be a living testimony that Jesus dwells in his heart. Do we have the power of the Spirit of God in our grasp? Are we good stewards for Christ?

1/5/1969

"Now you have sorrow, but your sorrow will be turned into joy for I will see you again and your heart shall rejoice, and that joy no one can take from you." —John 16.20-22

God's gracious purposes are revealed in Jesus Christ, His well-beloved Son. It is a purpose of love and is intended to bring joy into human hearts. Certainly, there is nothing that human beings so universally and ardently seek after as joy. But with countless thousands today joy is a "will o' the wisp" which they can never grasp. Yet the words of Jesus in our text show us that joy is attainable. How encouraging and comforting is the assurance that our Lord here brings. There is a joy for all believers in Jesus Christ. Jesus does not promise to believers exemption from the common sorrows of life. We must expect to experience distress and want, sickness, and suffering, affliction and pain, bereavement and death. But this promise of joy is ours if we are true believers in Jesus Christ. His holy Gospel brings us comforting assurance that He will not leave us or forsake us in an emergency in our earthly lives, but rather He will be ever with us to strengthen us in our weakness, to comfort us in our trials and troubles and deliver us from every evil work, and preserve us unto His heavenly Kingdom. Worldly and unbelieving persons may well despair when calamities overtake them or when death stares them in the face. They have no refuge to which they may cling for safety.

But how different it is with those who are believing Christians. Our joy is in our ever-present Lord and it is so deep that it enters the innermost recesses of our hearts, and so permanent that no one can take it away from us. The world cannot give such joy, nor can it take it away. Let us therefore never murmur or complain, but ever rejoice in the Lord, for through Him alone, everlasting life is possible.

Questions and Thoughts for Reflection

1. What should we think about "the baptism of the Holy Spirit"? This phrase has often been used to refer to some experience subsequent to conversion, but that is clearly not what Paul is talking about

in 1 Corinthians 12 when he says, "By one Spirit we have all been baptized into the one body and have been given the same Spirit from which we drink." Clearly, he is talking about conversion, the point at which we join the body of Christ, not some subsequent to conversion experience. And notice as well he is not talking about a baptism performed by a human being. He says the Spirit is doing this baptizing and he emphasizes it is absolutely essential to being a Christian. How very different these remarks are from what he says about water baptism in 1 Corinthians 1 where he actually exclaims, "I thank God I did not (water) baptize more of you." I cannot imagine Paul saying I thank God I did not convert more of you, or that more of you were not baptized by the Spirit.

It is true that we may have many spiritual experiences long after conversion—call them the second or third or fourth blessings if you like. But again, the phrase baptism in or of the Holy Spirit doesn't refer to those experiences. As the Pentecost event shows having the Spirit in your life is the *sine qua non* of being a Christian at all. And just as importantly, as my grandfather stresses, the Holy Spirit is a person, not merely a force or power or substance. You don't get the Holy Spirit in your life on the installment plan—some now, more later. Yes, the Spirit can get hold of more dimensions of your inner life over time—your will, your thoughts, your feelings, and that is called progressive sanctification. The Spirit can give you more understanding and guidance over time. But you can no more have a little bit of the Spirit in your life than a woman can be a little bit pregnant. Again, the Spirit is a person, not a thing, a force, or a substance. Either the person of the Spirit is in your life, or not. How have you thought about the Holy Spirit in the past? Have you made the mistake of thinking of the Spirit as merely divine power or anointing?

2. The second lesson for today works well with the first one, for the joy that is the subject of this lesson comes from the Holy Spirit. It is part of the fruit of the Spirit listed in Galatians 5 (love, joy, etc.). The fruit of the Spirit is about *character formation*, whereas the gifts of the Spirit are about *equipping for various sorts of ministry*. Everyone needs

the fruit of the Spirit, but not everyone needs one particular spiritual gift given by the Spirit.

The joy that comes from the Spirit is not like the joy that comes from some ordinary human experience or pleasure. Divine joy is something that the world can neither provide nor take away. It is a joy in the Lord. And interestingly and surprisingly it often shows up in the midst of trials, suffering, disease. There is a legend told about Christians being set on fire by Nero on crosses in Rome. The story goes that they begin singing even as they are dying, and this maddens Nero—he could not understand how they could sing joyful songs while dying. The joy of this lesson is about something that comes from the indwelling Spirit in a person's life not from external circumstances. Have you ever experienced this sense of joy, perhaps even in difficult times? Sometimes it is helpful to write down an account of such experiences so that you will remember them when challenges arise again. Have you ever kept a diary of your Christian experiences? Perhaps now is the time to start doing so because the older we get the more we forget.

Twenty-sixth Sunday of the Year

"Paul left Athens and went to Corinth where he met a Jew named Aquila and his wife Priscilla, because the Emperor Claudius had ordered all Jews out of Rome." —Acts 18.1-2

Paul went to see them and lived with them in Corinth. He worked with them in tentmaking and in spreading the Gospel. Later they returned to Rome. Priscilla and Aquila were real friends to Paul and risked their lives for him. And now, they were holding meetings in their home for there were no church buildings in that day. Thus, they met in small groups, and because of this the people became much closer to each other. Every home should be a miniature church today. Man and wife should have a mission to perpetuate a Christian home.

Paul warned the people about those whose intent and purpose was to destroy the fellowship. Paul told them to watch for and keep away from those determined to cause dissension in the church. He said they are false teachers with selfish motives. They are determined to cause trouble and deceive the people. Jesus said, "Beware of false prophets; you shall know them by their fruit." Paul shared his ministry with many wonderful people and felt that each of them had made a significant contribution to the fellowship.

What Paul is saying here is somewhat like the man who said that to be a good politician, a person must be able to straddle a fence and keep both ears to the ground at the same time! To be a Christian, a person cannot serve two masters, Jesus Christ and the Devil at the same time.

Christianity is a full-time job. If we are full-time Christians we will love our family and our fellow human beings and will not say things that are detrimental about our fellow human beings or try to encourage people to be mad with one another. The second commandment says we are to love our neighbor as ourselves. So, it behooves every Christian to always be alert for those who cause strife and disunity, who come to you in sheep's clothing but are actually wolves. They use all kind of tactics to cause dissension and disunity. Genuine Christian fellowship is one of the great joys of being a Christian. We are actually one in Christ and one in a family that we may share with each other the blessings of Christ.

7/7/68

"And I saw the dead, great and small, standing before the throne, and books were opened. Another book was opened, which is the book of life. The dead were judged according to what they had done as recorded in the books. The sea gave up the dead that were in it, and death and Hades gave up the dead that were in them, and each person was judged according to what they had done. Then death and Hades were thrown into the lake of fire. The lake of fire is the second death. Anyone whose name was not found written in the book of life was thrown into the lake of fire." —Revelation 20.12-15

"The books" are those that contain every act and every word good and bad of every individual person. However the Bible also talks about another book—"the book of life." The moment you receive Jesus Christ as Savior your name is removed from the "books" and transferred to the book of life. The Bible teaches that the blood of Jesus Christ, God's Son, cleanses us from all sin.

To the Christian, it is thrilling to know that God waits and listens in order to protect us. He watches over us probing our thoughts and conversations that He might help us. If we could see into the spiritual world, we would be conscious of the fact that God is involved in our daily lives for our protection. This is why the Scripture says, "Enter into his gates with thanksgiving and into his courts with praise." "Be thankful unto Him and bless his name. The Lord is good and his mercy is everlasting and his truth endures to all generations."

The great question we should ask ourselves today is, Is my name written in the book of life? Is my God material or spiritual? Today is the day of salvation, today is the day of grace. God watches, hears us, hoping we will accept His love and mercy and be saved. But a day of judgment is coming. Nothing escapes God's gaze. He hears all, knows all, sees all. Nothing would make Him happier than for us to accept Him. This is why the Scriptures say, "Be sure your sins will find you out." God's knowledge of us is complete, and his judgments are all sure. Notice that someone's name can first be in the book of life, and then be erased if he or she commits apostasy, rejecting the faith and the Christian way of life. Is your God spiritual or material?

Today God's mercy and love is extended to us, if we reject it we still must face the great day of judgment. Is your name written in the book of life? This concerns each of us individually for we must each account for our own sins. No one can do that for us. But fortunately, our Judge is also our Savior, and He desires that we all be saved.

Questions and Thoughts for Reflection

1. Sometimes Christians romanticize the early church and think if we could only get back to being like that all things would be well. Yet even a cursory reading of Acts or the letters of Paul suggest we should not idealize the early church in most respects. Most of Paul's letters are problem solving letters, and we have stories in Acts about people like Ananias and Sapphira, or even about sincere Christians like Paul and Barnabas who could not come to agreement about Mark going with them on a second missionary journey. The first lesson warns us about and against people who create division and dissension within the church. This seems to be a universal problem but it has especially plagued Protestants. It is frankly a scandal that there are now hundreds of Protestant denominations. When God said "be fruitful and multiply" to Adam and Eve, He did not mean create more denominations. All too often new denominations are the results of divisions and dissensions not a result of principled disagreements between equally mature Christians as was the case with the dispute between Paul and Barnabas, or even the one between Paul and Peter in Antioch.

1 John tells us that we must beware of wolves in sheep's clothing and then there are the chilling words "they went out from us, but they were not of us." And this in turn reminds us that just because someone is an official member of a church, that doesn't mean they are genuine Christians. Just because the mouse is in the cookie jar, it doesn't make him a cookie. So, what should a church do with a person who is causing all kinds of trouble and dissension in a church? Sometimes sadly, the minister has to ask them first to refrain from such contentiousness, and if it doesn't stop, then ask them to leave and go somewhere else. What has been your experience of such instances or even of whole church splits? What were the causes and the results? Was sin involved, or simply some practical disagreements (e.g., should we build this building?). Think about these things.

2. One thing that becomes clear about my grandfather from probing these lessons carefully. He was a freewill Baptist through and through. He didn't think you were eternally secure until you were securely in eternity. And as the lesson for today suggests, your name could be in the Lamb's book of life, and as Revelation says, it could also be erased from that book. Thirdly, my grandfather believed whole-heartedly that there is a complete record even of Christians words and deeds and that there will be a day of reckoning with Christ when He sits on the judgment seat. Pop is clear that salvation is by grace and through faith, but this does not mean there is not accountability for one's beliefs and behavior, and indeed even rewards for good behavior, for serving the Lord well (cf. what Paul says about his fellow ministers and how they build their ministry in 1 Cor 3). This orientation in his Christian life had as its naturally corollary that Pop believed he needed to be a straight arrow, live an upright life, confess his sins as needed and so on. He believed God was watching him all the time. The question is, are we likewise diligent about what we say and do? Do we realize that God requires more of the saved when it comes to accountability than He does of the lost? How would you evaluate your life on a day-to-day basis? Do you keep short accounts with God?

John Wesley set up band meetings for his Methodists in which they were expected at the end of each week to answer questions like: 1) What sins have you committed this week that you know of? 2) What things have you failed to do that you think may be a sin of omission? This approach was based on the verse in James about confessing our sins not to a minister or a priest but to each other. Such public confession of course creates its own accountability structure, because now your brothers and sisters are made aware of your weaknesses and missteps. I suspect if we followed this practice more frequently there would be less need for long exhortations from the preacher in the pulpit about sin.

Twenty-seventh Sunday of the Year

On Anger
4/24/77

Through God's will Paul was an apostle of Christ Jesus. He spoke to God's people in Ephesus telling them of God's grace and peace and His great love for humankind. God's plan was to bring all of creation together, in heaven and on earth with Christ as the head of it all.

The grace of God had given human beings a power which enabled them to die to sin and live righteously. We are warned not to let anger to cause us to sin. He said, "Yes it is human to show anger," but it should be controlled and not be allowed to cause us to do wrong, or unjust or injurious things to our fellow human beings. When we are severely criticized by others, we are not to respond in kind. Jesus was berated for healing a man on the sabbath and He was shocked when the disciples forbade the children to come to Him. He was angry when He cleansed the temple, and showed there is such a thing as righteous anger. He was righteously angry about inhumanity and hypocrisy. But there are unrighteous sorts of anger too.

Paul says put away all your bitterness and malice and be kind to one another. Be forgiving even as God for Christ's sake has forgiven us. One must be responsive to the clearest light we have and that is the great commandment about loving God and others and the ten commandments. Before we make decisions involving others we should ask, What would Jesus do in this situation? Jesus models for us the difference between righteous anger and unholy malice that seeks to harm or even destroy other human beings.

2/9/75

"Now when they saw the boldness of Peter and John and perceived that they were not learned or scholarly men they remembered that they had been with Jesus." —Acts 4.1

This of course applied to all twelve of the inner circle of Jesus. They learned much while accompanying the Master. They saw Him as independent and superior to all ordinary human judgment. They had the memory of Him as He went to the cross and this steeled them to the task ahead. The memory of the Jesus who arose made the thorns a crown of radiance, the cross a sacrifice glorified by courage and unwavering love. By the power of his memories Peter stood firm, at last "the rock," for Jesus called him Cephas which means rock. Peter would go on to say that "we ought to obey God rather than human beings" when he was told not to teach in Jesus' name or share His teachings (Acts 5.29). Peter not only defied the priests of the Sanhedrin who sought his life, he asserted three things: 1) his personal courage, 2) the moral imperative which distinguishes humans from lesser creatures, and 3) he asserted his allegiance to God. When we obey God rather than human beings our spirit becomes free.

Jesus said, "You shall know the truth and the truth will set you free." We must make this truth central in our thinking and in our allegiances. The Atlantic charter, pacts, treaties and the like, the whole range of political and economic contrivances will avail us not at all unless God's children stand firm in their loyalty to God. Where the spirit of the Lord is, there is true liberty. There is nothing this world needs as much as a clear appreciation of this fact. *The world is full of brave men and women who can face anything and everything except themselves.* A real facing up to ourselves is not the easiest thing in the world to do. It reveals too many unpleasant facts.

When we would do good, evil is present with us. The brave man faces himself, sees himself as he is, and asks—What can I do about it? Pilate refused to face himself, washed his hands of responsibility for Jesus' death and followed the path of least resistance. Paul faced himself on Damascus Road saying, "Lord what would you have me do?" We would do well to cultivate that ultimate heroism—the bravery that faces self each day and goes on in Christ's strength towards the victory over self. We must win that battle if we are to truly serve Christ.

Questions and Thoughts for Reflection

1. How does a Christian tell the difference between righteous anger and malice? When does the advice "be angry but sin not" come into play? The thing about anger is that it can cause a person to lose control. It can lead to spousal abuse. It can lead to judgmentalism of others that is not based in knowledge, but rather in assumptions. When Jesus said judge not lest you be judged by the same measure you judge others, He was not encouraging us to not be morally discerning about things. He was encouraging us to lead with compassion and understanding and forgiveness where needed just as He did during His ministry. Certainly, one of the worst spectacles is to see Christians firing angry verbal bullets at one another in a church meeting.

I was in the midst of such an occurrence already in my first year of ministry. Two committed families to one of my churches were suddenly yelling at each other because in both cases the parents wanted their children to lead the choir and the music program of that church. They erupted in the midst of an otherwise rather ordinary meeting, and the little old lady sitting next to me kept saying, "This is terrible, this is terrible." Once they had finishing hollering at each other, at least they didn't turn into the Hatfields and the McCoys. One of the families left the church, and it was a quite small church that needed every member it had. The church limped on wounded for a good while. Such is the damage unrighteous anger can do in the church. I tried to have the families reconcile but that feud had been building up for too long, and I didn't know all the back story.

Perhaps you also have seen such ungodly behavior at times in church. How was the matter dealt with and resolved, if it was? Do you think that some of the anger was justified or not? What is the difference between righteous anger, and malice?

2. Is your faith strong enough to stand severe criticism and respond graciously while standing firm on your convictions? This is one of

the key questions the second lesson raises for us. But as my grandfather says, sometimes it is easier to face any and all sorts of external criticism and challenges, but it is difficult and sometimes almost impossible to look in the mirror and face one's own faults honestly. Pop puts it this way: *The world is full of brave men and women who can face anything and everything except themselves.* Amen to that. But is your church also full of such people? Unfortunately, and precisely because church can involve strong emotions including in worship itself, sometimes egotism comes to the fore, including on the platform during worship. It is a sad spectacle. Remember the story of the Pharisee and the tax collector and which one went away justified in the sight of God? You would think that ministers especially need to regularly take their humility pills before performing their duties.

Interestingly, the discussion of humility in the New Testament does not have to do with feelings we have about ourself, but rather about behavior—humbling ourselves as Christ Himself did in the incarnation (Phil 2.5-11). Christ was not a person who suffered from feelings of low self-worth, and the humility discussed in Phil. 2 has to do with stepping down and serving others, with humbling ourselves to do even the most menial of tasks, like when Jesus washed His disciples' feet. Are you willing to humble yourself not only in the sight of the Lord but in the presence of your fellow believers? Are you brave enough to face yourself and your foibles?

Twenty-eighth Sunday of the Year

4/4/76

"So Jesus said to the twelve, 'Do you want to go away as well?' Simon Peter answered him, 'Lord, to whom shall we go? You have the words of eternal life, and we have believed, and have come to know, that you are the Holy One of God.'" —John 6.67-69

While instructing the disciples on events to come, Jesus told them some four times after Peter's confession at Caesarea Philippi that He would be put to death like a criminal and then rise again and be with them for a period of time. In the context of John 6 we hear that many had taken offense at Jesus' hard sayings and had turned away and so Jesus quite naturally asked if the Twelve would abandon Him as well. Peter's answer is given in the text read for today.

Later Jesus was carried before the Sanhedrin and was asked, "Are you the Son of the Blessed?" to which Matthew reports He replied, "You say that I am." Then the council said we need no witnesses, He is condemned by His own words. So, then He was taken before Pilate, was tried, and nothing was found against Him. Then (according to Luke) Pilate, finding out Jesus was from Galilee, sent Him to Herod Antipas who had a residence in Jerusalem for visits during the festivals. Herod had his soldiers try in every possible way to make Jesus perform some miracle, but He would not. Herod also found nothing against Jesus and sent Him back to Pilate. Pilate, following a custom of releasing a prisoner at the festival, offered the assembled crowd a choice between Barabbas, a known violent revolutionary, and Jesus. The crowd said "Give us Barabbas," and so Pilate set Him free. Finally,

Pilate washed his hands of the matter and handed the judgment of Jesus over to those who cried crucify Him, though only he had the authority of capital punishment and his own men had to carry out the gruesome deed.

They took two other bandits along with Jesus to Golgotha and made Jesus carry His own cross beam. On the way there, women were weeping and wailing for Him, seeing the severe punishment the Romans were inflicting on Him, and He responded, "Cry for yourself," meaning this very thing could happen to them. After He was nailed to the cross, the soldiers even gambled for His clothes, and some continued to mock and torment Him, and yet after all this Jesus said, "Father forgive them for they know not what they do." One of the two revolutionaries on the crosses beside Him said to Him, "If you are so powerful, then save yourself and us!" The other one, perhaps repenting of his evil deeds said 'when you come into your kingdom, remember me Jesus' He knew that Jesus was not guilty of any wrong, but knew that He Himself was, and in essence was asking to be forgiven and saved. Jesus amazingly replied, "Amen, I say to you, today you will be with me in Paradise," by which He meant heaven. Jesus then dropped His head on His shoulder and died, saying, "Father into thy hands I commend my spirit."

It is hard to understand, but Jesus had the real weight of the world on His shoulders, for He was accounted guilty for your sins and mine. We are the ones who have broken God's laws. The cross of Christ is a challenge to every generation, saying to us, "You are guilty, you are wrong." But will we listen?

2/14/71

"Seek ye first the Kingdom of God, and his righteousness, and all these things shall be added to you." —Matthew 6.33

With all the problems of life surrounding us today, our Lord gives us one guiding principle of action. God has a kingdom which is central in His thought—a kingdom of souls. We were created to honor, love, and obey Him. The nature of His kingdom was revealed in the life, the teaching, the character, and the death of our Savior on the cross. It is the kingdom of righteousness, truth, and peace.

Against this kingdom the powers of evil are always fighting, in the heart, the city, the state, and the world. Sin represents a great revolt throughout the world, against the divine rule of Christ and is the cause of the misery of the human race. Every one of us is called and it is our duty to take the side of God in the contest by putting His kingdom first of all, in all our decisions and in all our life. We must seek it first in order of choice-- God must come before pleasure, politics, or personal gain. God at the heart of life will purify and ennoble every relationship, and will pave the way toward the golden era in which people, loyal to the King, who is also our Father, will be brothers and sisters of one another. War, religious persecution, and selfish competition in daily life will all be impossible when the first thought of men, is to do the will of God. This seems a far off ideal today, but every life devoted to Jesus Christ in the power of love kindled at Calvary helps to bring it nearer. The great prayer will yet find an answer—thy Kingdom come, thy will be done on earth as it is in heaven.

Questions and Thoughts for Reflection

1. There are some hard sayings of Jesus that have led some in antiquity and some today to turn away from Jesus. Peter however responded properly, "To whom else shall we go? You have the words of everlasting life." Throughout the Gospels and particularly in the Gospel of John the message is that "no one comes to the Father accept through the Son." He is both the medium and the message of being born again and having everlasting life—the way, the truth, the life. Of course, this message offends modern religiously pluralistic cultures, indeed it even offends some Christians who try to whittle off the hard edges of the Gospel.

But at the bottom of this is a failure to recognize just how unique Jesus was and is. He is the only God-man, who could both represent humanity to God and vice versa. He is the only mediator of that sort in all of human history and He alone could provide redemption because of this fact. Jesus is the only person for whom Jesus did not need to die! 1 Tim. 2.5-6 is quite clear there is one God the Father and one mediator between God and humanity, Jesus Christ who provided the unique, once for all ransom for lost humanity so that all may be saved. I doubt, if someone had a terminal illness and there was only one doctor in the world who knew how to cure it, we would be complaining why aren't there multiple options, multiple persons we could go to? I think we would be getting on a plane and going to see that one doctor. Well, Jesus is the one and only person who qualifies as the great saver of human beings both because of who He is and because of His unique abilities to do what He has done and will do. Sometimes this message is called the scandal of the Gospel, a stumbling block to some, an outrageous assertion to others. Do you know people who make these sorts of objections to the Gospel? How would you respond to them?

2. What exactly is this Kingdom, which according to Jesus is "not of this world" that we are supposed to be seeking first? And first before what? And what exactly is Jesus talking about when He says if we do so, all sorts of things will be added to us. In context, it seems clear Jesus doesn't mean all the material possessions we could possibly dream of. The context in Matthew 5–7 suggests He is talking about food, clothing, and shelter—the basic necessities of life, which God provides for other creatures as well. Part of our problem is the very word kingdom. We always associate that with a place, but in fact when Jesus says things like "if I cast out demons by the Spirit of God you will know the *malkuta of God* has broken into your midst," He is referring to God's divine saving activity resulting in God's reign in a person life instead of Satan ruling it. In other words, he's talking about a reign, not a realm. So the saying really means "seek first the divine saving activity and its results in human lives and then . . . other things will be added."

Twenty-ninth Sunday of the Year

Angels
2/1/76

We are hearing a lot these days about our nation's secret agents—the CIA, some good and some bad. Today I want to talk about God's secret agents—the angels. They deal with the spiritual and supernatural while we deal with the natural, with mundane human experience. Yet we are limited so far as contact is concerned. God has given the angels a higher knowledge than ours. In the angelic realm the limitations are different from those God has imposed on our natural order. He has given angels not only higher knowledge but also high power and mobility than He has given us.

Have you ever seen or met one of these superior beings called angels? They are God's messengers and that is even what the word *aggelos* means in Greek. Their chief business is to carry out God's orders in the world. He has designated and empowered them as holy deputies to perform works of righteousness. Some people would have us believe they are only spiritual will-o'-the-wisps. Angels apparently have the ability to change their appearances and go in a flash from the glory of heaven to earth and back again. We must realize that these are non-material ministering spirits to humankind.

Angels are everywhere and are appointed to special tasks by God, who is able to have them take visible form if He so desires. There are thousands and thousands of them, and we shall know more about them in the future. They are of utmost importance to us. The Bible states that angels, like human beings, were created by God, and Paul says they are in heaven and on earth, visible and invisible, created by and for Jesus Christ who was and is before all things, and by Him all things consist, so that even angels would cease to exist if Jesus Christ, as the second person of the Trinity, did not sustain them by His power.

Luke 10.25-37
6/8/75

There was a man who had wrecked his car and was lying on the ground, but no one seemed to want to stop and help him. One man saw the situation and said to himself 'I cannot stop. I don't have time to be a witness in court, and another passing on by said 'I don't want to be involved and went on. After several people had passed on by, finally a man stopped and helped the man taking him to the hospital and turned him over to the interns, leaving his name and telephone number, so that if the injured man needed him for any reason, he would help all he could. How many people today avoid helping their fellow human beings who are in need? So many people fail to help a neighbor in trouble for no good reason at all. They don't seem to care or perhaps don't realize that it could have been themselves in need of a neighborly act.

Most people today are too selfish or self-absorbed to have a feeling of brotherly love. If we, each of us, just stop and think how much our lives really depend on other people, even for the very necessities of life such as food, shelter, and clothing we might act differently. Despite what Cain said, we really are our brother's keeper. How often do we realize we are violating the first and second commandment in our failure to aid our neighbor in his misfortunes. What kind of person would you want to come along if you were in trouble? Surely not the man that doesn't have the time or the one who doesn't want to be involved. I am sure you would want the man who was kind enough to help in whatever way the future might demand.

Last year I had a wreck at Fuquay-Varina, North Carolina. My wife was injured and hospitalized. The policeman who came to the scene took my wife to hospital and later took me over there, and I found out he missed church because of my accident. After my wife was examined, the doctor wanted her to go to the hospital in Raleigh for pictures. The rescue squad took us there and we discovered the two men on the truck were both Sunday school teachers. The police, for his part, recommended a man to repair my car, and later I found out that he was the chairman of the Board of Deacons in the Baptist Church. I was well pleased with the job and more than pleased with the treatment we received. I thank God for people who care enough to do something about it when a fellow human being needs help.

[The previous story is about my grandparents coming to Chapel Hill on Sunday, May 12, 1974, for my college graduation ceremony. It was a rainy day. They never arrived, and later we heard the rest of the story in an age before texting, mobile phones, and the like.]

Questions and Thoughts for Reflection

1. Do you believe in angels? For some reason, many people find it easier to believe in angels than to believe in God, even though they are both supernatural beings. Still other people attribute to saints, like Saint Anthony, the idea of where divine help comes from when we need it. I don't have any problem with the saints in heaven being given jobs by God, but the Bible doesn't mention it, and it says quite a lot about God's secret agents—angels. The texts which we have suggest they can move between the material and spiritual universes at will, and also suggest that they can appear in human forms that we would not necessarily find threatening. Mainly they are God's messengers but there are also said to be various sorts of guardian angels, for example for God's chosen people. Angels tend to show up to announce big things in the salvation plan of God, and so not surprisingly we find them in the Gospel birth and resurrection stories, but not so much elsewhere. To judge from Isaiah 6 and Revelation, angels are part of the heavenly court and part of the worship team, among other things.

Satan seems to have been part of that heavenly court as the prosecuting attorney whose job was to test and/or tempt human beings like Job or Jesus, and of course others. Revelation suggests he was kicked out of heaven, and so does Jesus who mentions His seeing Satan fall like lightning from the heavens. The angels in Gen. 6 are called 'sons of God' and as the story (and its replay in Jude and 2 Peter) suggests, they are capable of wickedness as well as good. In other words, like human beings they have free will or at least the power of contrary choice. The Biblical story suggests God's plan includes Christ ruling over all the principalities and powers as well as over human beings and the material creation we call the universe.

What should we think about all of this? For one thing, angels remind us that we are not the only creatures God has made. God's focus in the end is on all creatures great and small and the redemption of all that He created. Finally, what should we think of the angel of death in the Exodus story, or the angels who implement the judgments of the seven seals, trumpets, and bowls? What is interesting about all of that is none of those judgments are final judgment. They are not in the main punitive, but rather disciplinary, with God hoping for repentance and a return to fellowship with God. Final judgment is left in the hands of Christ Himself . . . and thank goodness that is so, for He is also our Savior. What do you make of Christ's dual role of Final Judge and Savior?

2. The story of the Good Samaritan has long resonated with Christians, even to the point of Augustine turning the story into an allegory with Christ as the Good Samaritan, the Inn as the church, the coins as penance money and so on. In fact, the story is about none of that. It is about kindness, and self-sacrificial helping of those in need even when the person you are helping mighty be seen as at best a rival, and at worst an enemy. Such was the case with Samaritans and Jews in Jesus' day, and He is trying to deconstruct that social divide and animosity. My grandfather uses the story to illustrate both the propensity of fallen persons towards selfish and self-protective behavior, and yet at the same time the possibility of human goodness even in surprising situations. He tells the story of why he never got to my college graduation, but was helped by various Baptist good Samaritans.

Who are the surprising good Samaritans in your life? Can you recount an episode in your life when someone came to the rescue completely unexpectedly and perhaps out of character? What do such incidents tell you about the possibility for human kindness, help, and even love? The story after all is told in response to the lawyer wanting a narrow definition of who counts as a neighbor so he can know who he is obligated to help. Jesus instead tells a story about how we should be good neighbors to whoever needs our help.

Thirtieth Sunday of the Year

2 Kings 6
11/30/75

In the sixth chapter of 2 Kings we read about a man chopping down trees to build a house. While he was chopping he lost the ax head off the handle so he had to quit. He couldn't cut down trees with an ax handle. Do you know what a lot of us are doing? We've lost our cutting edge, but still are chopping with the handle and getting nowhere. We are trying to win souls, trying to live a Christian life, trying to produce the fruit of the Spirit with something that cannot accomplish that.

We don't need a new organization, we need to ask are you filled with the Holy Spirit? Our desperate need is not for a new organization or even a new movement or a new method. We have enough of these. The greatest need is that men and women that profess Jesus Christ be filled with the Holy Spirit. If you are not, you are sinning against God. You have no victory in your life, no thrill, no brilliancy. You may say "I want to be filled, I want joy in my life. I want to produce the fruit of the Spirit. I don't want to be up one day and down the next. I want to live on the peak of God's grace and love. I want to shine for Christ as a radiant Christian." But then you have to ask yourself—Do you really mean it? If you really do, then you can be filled with the Holy Spirit. But it costs something. There is a price to pay. Are you willing to pay for an abundant life? On the authority of the Word of God, it is available to every man, woman, and child in Christ.

We must first be cleansed from sin, we must confess our sins of omission—our ingratitude, our lack of love for Christ, our neglect of the Word, unbelief, lack of prayer, failure to attend church service, lack of feeling for lost souls, neglect of family duties, lack of friendliness to others, refusing to deny ourselves. All of these are sins. Then we need to confess our sins of commission—worldliness, pride, envy, a bitter spirit, holding grudges, slander, gossiping, lying, cheating, hypocrisy, robbing God, temper, malice. All these have to be confessed, renounced, and put away.

The next step is consecration. To sum up in a few words what victorious living is I would say yielding all to God, letting God have His way in every phase of my life. Consecration is simply surrender. If we try to keep some secret sin, never yield it or surrender it, we never know what real consecration is. Remember God is all wise, He knows even our every thought or feeling. Are you holding out or holding back on God? If so, you must pay the penalty. If we are guilty of one sin, we are guilt of all until we have repented. Today is the day of salvation. All that are and all that we have belong to God.

8/23/70

"These are the ones who have turned the world upside down and now have come here." —Acts 17.6

This passage is suggestive of God's purpose and His method of securing its fulfillment. The Gospel is truly a revolutionary force. *It turns things upside down in order to make them stay right side up. In the sphere of individual life this is what conversion means. The reborn soul radically changes its government by dethroning itself and enthroning Christ.* In all our social institutions—the family, the church and the state—the renewed men and women make the new community by overturning the powers of evil and establishing over them the kingdom of righteousness, peace and joy in the Holy Spirit. The Gospel is a universally operating force. It knows no boundaries of longitude or latitude. It is spreading as the Savior said it would, to the uttermost parts of the earth. It has the promise and potency of worldwide dominion. It can and does meet the needs of all, however some of us fail to understand this.

Every continent on the globe can now, by way of praising our ecumenical missionary enterprise, also use the very words of that false indictment of those Jews of Thessaloniki against Paul and Silas: "these who have turned the world upside down have come hither." And also, the Gospel is a humanly conditioned force. It works through the faith and love of those who accept its teachings and incarnates them in their daily life—divine truth shining through human personalities. This is the secret of the success of Christianity as a revolutionary and universally operative force in human history. Christ works through Christians. Is He working through you?

Questions and Thoughts for Reflection

1. In the first lesson for this Sunday, my grandfather wants to talk about what gets in the way of our being full of the Spirit and effective joyful witnesses. He points to how sin gets in the way of that sort of abundant and victorious Christian living. There are many things that get in the way of our witness, both sins of commission and sins of omission as well. Sometimes we mistakenly think that if we haven't committed any major sins then we must be alright, but then we don't understand why we don't have more joy in our lives and power in our witness. Confession is not just good for our souls, it's good for our ability to witness effectively as well.

What are the things that may be getting in the way of your being a Spirit-filled joyful and powerfully witnessing Christian person? Are you afraid of offending others? Afraid of rejection because of being such an overt Christian person? I am not suggesting we should be obnoxious for Jesus and get in the faces of people totally unreceptive and unprepared to hear the Gospel. You have to have some spiritual discernment to know when and how to share the message and with whom. What are the things getting in the way of the fruit of the Spirit being fully manifest in your life, and ask yourself this: is there evidence in your life that you are a more patient, more joyful, more loving Christian than you were a year ago? If not, why not?

2. We live in a world where things are often backwards or upside down, and not in a good way. But our second lesson for today is talking about turning the world upside down in a good way, in a better way, turning it away from its downward spiral. More specifically

these remarks have to do with the fact that early Christianity was in some way countercultural. Christians would not worship the gods of this world or the emperor, would not go along with various cultural practices such as going to dinner parties in pagan temples where the pagan god or goddess was the host and was honored at the meal.

They were seen as anti-social, indeed they were even called *atheoi*, literally without gods, a term from which we get the word atheist, because they refused to honor the traditional Greek and Roman deities, as well as their own Biblical God. Then too they believed in a heavenly commonwealth or governmental center of their lives— Christ was Lord over them and His Kingdom, not the kingdoms of this world, was what really mattered. No wondered people like Paul and His converts were seen as subversive of the fabric of society, of the extant world order. But have we lost this orientation altogether? Have we become domesticated serving both God and Mammon? Have we allowed the world to conform us into its mold rather than seeking to transform the world? While our money says "in God we trust," it often seems we trust our money more than our God, or our military prowess on which we spend billions more than we trust God. What is wrong with this picture? How would you view it?

Thirty-first Sunday of the Year

7/21/68

"The eyes of the LORD run to and fro throughout the whole earth, to show himself strong in the behalf of them whose heart is perfect towards Him." —2 Chronicles 16.9

A statesman tells of his experience in prison. In the door of his room there was a small hole through which a soldier peered night and day. Every time the statesman glanced towards the door he saw that eye. It was a terrible experience. I was taught by a Sunday school teacher that the eye of God was always upon me, watching to see if I did anything I ought not to do. I was told all my naughtiness was recorded in the great book of judgment.

How different is the tone of this text from 2 Chronicles. The eyes of the Lord are against the wicked, but they are with the righteous. Righteousness is an attitude not an attainment. What a trinity of blessing is this text—the wings of the Almighty, the everlasting arms of love, and the light of His countenance. The wicked may live within the health-giving light of His countenance. The eyes of the Lord never fail us. They penetrate every experience and enlighten every week of life.

To go back to my boyhood days, I recall going out to the woodshed for some wood. The night was black and I would have been terribly afraid had it not been for my mother who stood in the kitchen door. Her eyes were upon me. That assurance brightened my darkness. So it is with the deeper experiences of human living—the consciousness that God is with us in everything. That is Christianity and the supreme message of Christ. He came that we might have life and have it abundantly and eternally. Are we following Him? His eyes are upon us wherever we go and in whatever we do. He knows even our innermost thoughts.

6/29/69

"I call upon heaven and earth to witness against you this day that I have set before you life and death, blessing and curse. Therefore, choose life that you and your descendants may live, loving the Lord your God, obeying his voice, and cleaving to Him for that means life to you and length of days, that you may dwell in the land which the Lord swore to your fathers—to Abraham, Isaac, and to Jacob to give them." —Deuteronomy 30.19-20

Our Scripture for today is very impressive. Moses is calling upon the children of Israel to choose the way of life instead of the way of death. On every day, we are choosing either the narrow way that leads to life eternal, or the broad and easy way that leads to destruction.

A woman of our day put this appeal to choose life in these words: "Never forget to live. We can forget to live if we do not watch and pray. We can become absorbed in the outside details of living so that we forget to live in the highest sense—the life of fellowship with God, and of helpful fellowship with people. We should continually ask God to save us from the blunder of grasping the material things of life and missing the life of God in our souls."

But I am afraid there are too many of us that are careless and unconcerned. We use the expression "as far as I am concerned" and we say it in all sorts of connections. We say "as far as I am concerned it would be alright if I never had any carrots" or "as far as I am concerned I have no desire to fly." But let's put the question this way—How much are you concerned about the things that make for the betterment of your city, your country, your world, indeed your own life? How much are you really concerned about the progress of your church? About racial injustice and racial conflicts? About the homeless refugees of the world? About the peace of the world?

You say "as far as I am concerned," but just how far is that? How wide is our concern for God's family, our fellow human beings? Does it match the wideness of God's mercy to us? Are we in the end willing to bear each other's burdens?

Questions and Thoughts for Reflection

1. Perhaps at some point you have heard the famous spiritual that says "His eye is on the sparrow, and I know He watches me." The Scripture for this lesson has that same sort of positive message. If you just say God will be watching you, that often has a negative connotation like the song by Sting that says "Every breath you take/ every move you make/ every step you take I'll be watching you." It is a song about a voyeur or a stalker. But not so our text for today. It would be better to say the text refers to the fact that God is watching out for us. The message is His providential care for us, not something negative.

My wife recently had a remarkable and rather scary situation. She was sitting at an intersection and the light had already turned green but something told her to wait, and she froze for minute—just in time to see a truck barreling through the red light at high speed. That hesitation may have saved her life. We both thought that was God watching out for her. So often we are completely oblivious to the dangers that are around us because we can't see them at first glance. But God sees them. If His eye is on the sparrow, we can be sure He also watches out for us and cares what happens to us. How about you? Have you had experiences in life, perhaps narrow misses in a dangerous situation, which caused you to sense the presence of a God who looks after His children? Take a little time and write down one or more of these experiences, and then if you have a day of doubts about God's care, go back and read what you wrote, and find some assurance.

2. How far does your concern about life stretch? Only as far as your immediate family? To your immediate and church family? To your family and all true Americans? To the Christians around the world? Or how about to the audience God cares about—the whole world? Not only does God care about the whole world, He loves the world

of humanity as is shown by His sending His Son to save the world. He did not come just to save a select few, He came to live and die for all of us and give us a chance to be redeemed. There is a wideness in God's mercy. But what about ours? How much concern do we have for those suffering elsewhere in the world from hunger, from living in a war-ravaged country?

Sometimes we are concerned for a short period of time because it is in front of us or on the news, but then our concern wanes and we turn our attention to other things. In the challenge from Moses in the second lesson for today, Moses tells his people that even everyday decisions that we make can affect our eternal outcome. In one sense, every day we have an opportunity to choose the path that leads to life or to choose the path that leads to outer darkness. We cannot afford to be cavalier about life, not least because much is on the line even in small decisions. There is a famous saying that goes as follows: "for want of a nail, the horseshoe was lost, for want of the shoe the horse was lost, for want of the horse the battle was lost, for want of the battle the war was lost, and all because of the lack of a nail." Little things add up, so keep choosing life, and remember your choices are not value free. They matter.

Thirty-second Sunday of the Year

10/20/68

"If my people who are called by my name shall humble themselves and pray and seek my face and turn from their wicked ways, then will I hear from heaven and will forgive their sins, and will heal their land." —2 Chronicles 7.14

Centuries ago, God spoke these words to the Hebrew people. Theirs was a history of constantly falling into sin and endeavoring to pull themselves up by their own bootstraps. They were no more able to accomplish this feat than we are today. In a particular way, America has been a nation whose God was the Lord. Our forebears came here seeking political and religious freedom. The course of events in the world for the last fifteen years has demonstrated beyond a shadow of a doubt that political liberty goes hand in hand with religious liberty. Lose the one and it is not long before you lose the other.

Because of our reliance upon God, we have been singularly blessed by Him, and as in the case of the ancient Hebrews our very prosperity has produced an overweening pride. Just a few short years ago we condemned the English for their dole instead of recognizing the evils of our own economic system that would soon bring the dole our way. Statesmanship for our nation reached the lowest mark of the twentieth century when we were promised prosperity on a beer and alcohol wave, then came the drug and addiction problem. Today we see the fruits of our folly, hopefully. Prosperity is not as far off as it once was, our youth are debauched, and our streets and highways are not safe. As it turns out, material prosperity is not the be all and end all of existence. Indeed, it can even spoil us and corrupt us.

While there are many ills to be cured, the greatest need of the modern world is to confess its sins, repent, and turn back to God. Then and only then can we have a world that is fit to live in. It is time to realize we are drifting into anarchy and that we should say as Jesus did, "get behind me Satan," and be very sure that we are born again.

8/11/68

"Son of man, say unto the prince of Tyre, thus says the Lord: Because you have lifted up your heart, and you have said 'I am a god, I sit in the seat of god in the midst of the seas,' yet you are but a human being and not God though you have set your heart as the heart of God." —Ezekiel 28.2

The tragedy of our age is the attempt on the part of humankind to live as if there was no God. But human beings remain only human and not God. For a generation or more, human confidence in ourselves has been growing and our trust in God has diminished. Human increase in knowledge, our scientific accomplishments, our power over nature almost convinced us that we have no further need of God. Humankind has come to feel that by our own wisdom and power we can master any personal, social, or world situation that may arise. But with all our boasting in our wisdom and unlimited power, with all our inventions and mechanisms, we have brought our world to chaos and impending ruin with world war after world war. Until human beings begin to despair of being able to find salvation in mere human resources and turn by the millions in every land to God for help, things will not be moving in the right direction. Perhaps in the spiritual atmosphere created by our supplications a new world may seem to be in the making.

When we have sincerely cried out to God in any age, He has always heard and saved humankind. This is the lesson of history. But God also needs the help of human beings, for without that God's purposes can be frustrated. If human beings are faithless and rebellious, his plans remain unfinished, unfulfilled. Only with the help of

God can human beings achieve our destiny, and only with the help of human beings will God's eternal purpose be fully realized, for that is the way God set up the world—with creatures, angelic and human that have a modicum of freedom of choice.

Only by and through God can we hope to gain peace in the world and everlasting life, The existence of a powerful God and the miracles He is able to perform are well beyond our abilities. There are many things we cannot understand about His purpose for us. This is where we must completely trust in Him with a knowledge that He is able to meet our every need, whatever it may be. We must follow Him. For there is only one true and powerful God, all others are false.

Questions and Thoughts for Reflection

1. Too few Christians think about the conditional nature of many of God's promises, and that includes the text for our first lesson for this Sunday. God has chosen to set up His universe in such a way that He relates to His human and angelic creatures in a personal way. He does not treat them as if they were inanimate pawns on a chess board to be moved around solely on the basis of His own choices. Rather, He treats them as beings that have their own choices to make. God gives His grace and love freely, and He wants us to freely respond positively and in love. And this includes responding with repentance when the occasion requires it and God calls for it. And in this very text we are reminded that God Himself responds to our own positive responses to His call for repentance. The conditional promise given here is that God will hear our cries, will forgive our sins, and will heal our land.

My grandfather contrasts this with how politicians often make promises of prosperity, but the promise is based on a sin tax, or the allowing of things that are bad for us to be sold in our country. Most recently our country has been legalizing the sale of a psychotropic drug called marijuana not merely for medicinal purposes but for recreational use. The problem with this is that the drug dulls the senses, and makes a person less alert, less able to function properly on the job, and worse. I once worked with a person who came to work stoned most every day. It was like he was moving and working in slow motion. The results were not good and he had to be let go.

What sort of price is our country paying for trying to legalize various forms of sin and bad practices that make our nation less productive? Will we heed the call to repent of all the things that get in the way of our being in right relationship with God, and being good citizens of our land? How would you evaluate the moral state of our country?

2. The second lesson pursues these same sorts of themes. Notice the stress on the fact that God has chosen to depend on us, His creatures, to implement His will on earth. Doubtless God could have done things differently but He wanted for us to relate to Him and His will in love which requires some freedom to respond positively. He wanted us to be His co-workers in the grand project of redeeming a lost world. What He did not want is for us to pretend we are gods, and we have no need of a heavenly Father. As Rom. 1.18-32 makes clear, this sort of approach to life amounts to a denial not only of God's existence but also of our own natures—namely that we were created in God's image and that we do actually know there is a powerful Creator God as it is evident in all His creation. Paradoxically, the denial of the existence of God amounts to a denial of our essential nature and ongoing identity. My grandfather puts it this way: "Only with the help of God can human beings achieve their destiny, and only with the help of human beings will God's eternal purpose be fully realized, for that is the way God set up the world—with creatures, angelic and human that have a modicum of freedom of choice."

Why do you think God set up the world this way? While I would not suggest that it was because God was lonely and needed love, I do think it has something to do with God's desire to relate to His creatures in a loving way, and desiring for them to freely receive this love, and freely respond to it. God wants personal relationships with us and with His angels as well. But there is more. There is no possibility of human virtue, of freely making moral choices, of choosing to imitate Christ if in fact there is no power of contrary choice. Indeed, there is no freely fulfilling the great commandment, no loving in the Biblical sense, without some grace enabled power of making meaningful choices in life. Does this explanation help you to understand why God has constructed His moral universe the way He has?

Thirty-third Sunday of the Year

9/26/79

"Before the mountains were brought forth, or even you had formed the earth, even from everlasting to everlasting thou art God."
—Psalm 90.2

Many people who do not read much and perhaps who never read the Bible ask questions about God. Where did He come from? Where does He live? Where is heaven? What does God look like? Has anybody ever seen God? By the very nature of things, there are many mysteries we cannot fully understand about God. Quite simply if God could be fully explained by human beings He wouldn't be the sort of all-knowing and all-powerful God who can help us.

God has always existed, the Bible tells us. He is eternal, and by His power He has created everything, even time itself. Consider the Psalm cited above. We human beings, bound as we are to this time and space cannot fully grasp this concept. However, because we cannot understand something, it does not mean it is not true. We use electricity every day, but we cannot fully explain it because we do not fully understand it. The fact that we do not fully understand it does not mean that it doesn't exist.

Although we may not understand all there is to know about God, we can still know God, having a personal relationship with Him. The wonderful thing is that God has invaded time. He loves humankind so much that He allowed Himself to become flesh in the person of Jesus Christ. And in the greatest event in the history of the universe, He took away our sins by allowing Himself to die on the cross.

We need not guess about the nature of God. God has shown His nature and His love for us by sending Christ into the world. "For God so loved the world that He gave His only begotten Son, that whoever believes in Him shall not perish, but have everlasting life, for God did not send His Son into the world to condemn the world, but that through Him the world might be saved" (John 3.16-17).

People who ask questions about God could satisfy their minds in many cases if they would only read and study the Bible, and discover how wonderful it is to be a child of God and to know what He has in store for all who repent and believe. He will accept you as you are, as the song goes, "Just as I am, without one plea, His precious blood was shed for me."

3/7/71

"Thus he has shown me and behold the Lord stood upon a wall made by a plumbline, with a plumbline in his hand. And the LORD said unto me 'Amos what do you see?' I said 'a plumbline./ Then the Lord said 'behold I will set my plumbline in the midst of my people Israel. I will not again pass by them anymore.' . . . and behold a basket of summer fruit. And he said 'Amos what do you see,' and I said 'a basket of summer fruit.' Then the LORD said unto me 'the end has come upon my people Israel. I will not again pass by them anymore.'" —Amos 7.7-8; 8.1-2

The destruction of the temple was imminent. The Lord had given them every chance to change their ways and repent. Amos was sent especially to Israel and he unleashed on those chosen people the full fury of his moral indignation. He first emphasizes the necessity of judgment. He says even Egypt and Philistia will be astonished at the destruction of the luxurious living in the palaces in Samaria, which the unrighteous accumulation of wealth had made possible. The ceremonial sins of Israel in their temple were merely evidence of a more serious problem. Worship offered by hands stained with sin, coming from hearts completely indifferent to the Lord's expectations, was unacceptable. Righteousness in relationship with one's fellow human beings is evidence of a righteous relationship with God.

Amos showed the Israelites how completely they had given themselves over to sensual gratification, confident that no judgment could reach them. They didn't recognize the Lord's real character and felt secure. The prophet gave a vision of judgment. He said "The Lord showed me," then he related the vast destruction by locusts and compared destruction by fire as of the same significance. The Lord was seen standing by a wall testing a plumbline. At this moment Amos realized all the irregularities the plumbline revealed, and the Lord declared the end had come. The vision of the basket of summer fruit also indicated the imminence of the judgment. The Lord did not completely destroy the temple, and later restored it to be used by those who were faithful to Him.

Today, God is giving us every chance to mend our ways, and He is continually warning of the consequences of not doing so, of being unfaithful, of our failure to love our fellow human beings and tell them of the Savior's great love for them and power to save. Do we measure up to God's plumbline today?

Questions and Thoughts for Reflection

1. One of the problems in having debates about the existence and nature of God is that there are limits to what human beings can really grasp or understand. Human beings are not omniscient, and there are things like the idea of an eternal anything, never mind an eternal being called God that is difficult to make sense of when everything around us and everything we are suggests it all has a time limit. It didn't always exist. My grandfather quite rightly stresses however that just because we cannot fully understand something doesn't mean it's not true. All too often human beings dismiss something out of hand as being pure fiction simply because they cannot comprehend it. In a universe full of surprises, human beings need to keep open minds, and this includes an open mind about God, although the famous humorous warning "don't be so open-minded that your brains fall out" is worth keeping in mind. Being open-minded doesn't mean being naïve or lacking in critical thinking about life.

For many of us, simply examining the complexity of nature, and the patterns that exist in it suggest that the world as we know could not have happened by chance or accident. Like the old saying suggests, if you find a watch you have to posit there is a watchmaker somewhere. The same applies when one sees the patterns and complexity in creation. It leads to the reasonable explanation that there must be a Creator. The important question however is what does examining creation tell us about the Creator? The answer is that it doesn't tell us enough to save us. We need not just the world of God to know God exists, we need the Word of God to reveal to us more fully God's character and His desire to love and rescue us from our own sins and stupidity.

It is not enough to know there is a Creator God. That doesn't solve some of our most fundamental problems in life. We need a savior and according to the Bible we need a savior that comes in person to rescue us. Nothing less will get the job done. To best understand a complex world and a complex God, one needs to read His Word. This raises the proper question: How much time do you spend in God's Word? My grandfather was largely self-taught when it came to the Bible and he must have spent thousands of hours investigating, learning, memorizing, and reflecting on God's Word—all of it. As these lessons show, he absolutely didn't limit himself to studying the New Testament as if that was all that mattered. How about you? Do you spend time reflecting on the Psalms or the so-called minor prophets like Amos?

Sometimes I start my Introduction to the New Testament class with a little test. I tell my students, "Please open your Bibles to the book of Hezekiah," and then I watch to see what happens. Now you must understand that my students are seminary students, not undergraduates. And alas, sometimes even half of them start thumbing through or clicking through their Old Testaments trying to find such a nonexistent book. Even many Christians do not adequately know God because they have not studied either His world or His Word in any detailed fashion. May these lessons not only nourish your soul but be a call to action. Will you take the time and energy to learn God's Word? You must if you want to better know God.

2. Amos was not just an oracular prophet. By this I mean he didn't just hear messages from God and then repeat them, he also had visions from God such as a vision of a basket of summer fruit, or a vision of a plumbline. The thing about visionary prophecy is that it requires extra interpretation. The only thing God says is He will not pass over or ignore their sins any longer. The plumbline image conjures up God's measuring His people (as well as their temple) and finding it 15 percent shy of plumb, or in other words, not measuring up to His standards. The imagery of the summer fruit, like the imagery of harvesting the wheat is frequently used to talk about a time of evaluation and judgment as to whether God's people have been fruitful or not, whether they have given God His due (wave offerings etc.) or not. These images come as warnings, but apparently Israel paid little or no attention to that prophet whose main job was as a plucker of figs! And then tragedy struck when the Assyrians came calling in 721 BC and destroyed much and took the leadership of Israel captive and carted them off to exile. Amos's warnings were ignored.

Sometimes we also ignore God's warnings that something bad can happen if we do not do something different. We ignore health warnings, we ignore highway warnings, we ignore governmental warnings, we ignore EPA warnings about climate change. Often, we are just as much a stubborn people not heeding God's warnings through various emissaries as the Israelites were. This lesson raises the question—What warnings have we ignored that we should have paid attention to? What things have we left undone that we should not have neglected? Are we aware that God is constantly taking our measure and evaluating our character, words, and deeds?

Thirty-fourth Sunday of the Year

4/27/69

"Everyone that thirsts, come to the waters, come, buy and drink, buy wine and milk without money and without price." —Isaiah 55.1

Suppose there would be an announcement in tomorrow's newspapers inviting you to come to a certain place and get a fortune with no expenditure on your part. Would you go? You would surely go if the integrity of the offer came from someone you trusted. God makes that kind of offer to His children—everything for nothing! His grace, His love, His salvation, and His heaven without money and without price to you. Only divine grace can invite us to come empty-handed and buy His precious gifts. It is an offer backed by the reality of God and the fully integrity of the divine character. That offer in Isaiah 55 has never been withdrawn. It has never failed of fulfillment. In giving this invitation God asks three things of us—he asks that we believe in Him and His invitation. Without faith, the invitation comes as a mockery. Faith assures us of the vital earnestness of God in making this offer. He also asks that we have a heart that is hungry and thirsty for His loving gifts. God will not bestow His gifts upon those who do not want them. He says "ask and you shall receive." We must also have the capacity to receive and use His blessings. He wants us to bring empty vessels to the fountain of divine grace. The only limitation upon our boundless possession of heaven's glories is our capacity to receive them. This is just like the oil that stopped flowing for the widow only when all the vessels were full.

Christian disciples are called to be witnesses for their Lord. Witnessing for Jesus is both a glorious privilege and a solemn responsibility. Multitudes of Christians who cannot speak publicly are testifying by the character of their Christian living. Are we prepared to receive this great fortune, and have we met the requirements? He gave His all for us, what will we do about the free gifts He is offering us?

4/8/73

"There is now no condemnation for those who are in Christ Jesus, because through Christ Jesus the law of the Spirit who gives life has set you free from the law of sin and death. And if Christ is in you, while the body is dead because of sin, the spirit is alive because of righteousness. If we have received the Spirit, we are children of God, joint heirs with Christ of everlasting life." —Romans 8.1-4

Through Christ we know what God is like because He is God the Son who came and lived among the people. He is as well the image of true humanity, showing what it really entails to be a true human being. Jesus needed to pray as we need to pray, however we need to pray much more for we are sinners and He was sinless. Jesus was always involved with people, doing wonders for them and at the same time showing them a way to life, a way to eternal bliss.

We must be like Jesus. You might retort, "Who, me?" Yes, you and me both because the Bible tells us that Jesus can actually share Himself with us. God's purpose for us is to give us a new nature, created after the likeness of God and in His holy righteousness. Paul often spoke of the Christian as being "in Christ." To know that He has received me into His own life and that someday I shall bear the very image of the resurrected Jesus, the man in heaven, is more than I deserve. Here is Christian identity. I came from God, I have been weak but He has sustained me in spite of my faults. And now my destiny is Jesus Christ.

Have you made this exciting discovery of identity in Christ? There are in fact three yous—the person you think you are, the person

God knows you are, and the person God knows you are becoming through Christ. What is your true identity with God?

Questions and Thoughts for Reflection

1. It has been said that you can't receive anything if you only hold out a closed fist. How open handed is your relationship with God? Have you been raised with the myth of self-sufficiency and believe you don't need much from God, don't even need much help in times of trouble? Sadly, many Christians have bought into our cultural lies about independence and self-sufficiency. As one preacher has said, "I don't believe in self-sufficiency, I believe in God sufficiency." Amen to that. God can do abundantly more than we could ever ask or even conceive. In our first lesson for today Isaiah reminds us that God is calling us to come to Him and receive what we need. In this case, the offer is of life sustaining food and beverages, something ancient peoples did not take for granted as we so often do.

When I give talks to children at schools I often ask them, "Where does food come from?" Their standard answer is "from the grocery store," not even "from the farm," and never once have I heard "from God." And yet the Bible is emphatic that all good gifts come from God. You have not because you ask not. But are you prepared to receive the help you need. Some of us are so proud of being apparently self-sustaining that we are too embarrassed to ask God for things we need. That sort of pride definitely goes before the fall. It gets in the way of our receiving what God wants to give us.

Take some time to do a personal inventory. What are the kinds of things you most need from God? Will you open your heart and hands and receive them? Sometimes it shows how little faith we have in God when we ask for something without expecting to receive anything and so are surprised or even shocked when it shows up! Is this you? If so, you need to place more trust in God.

2. It is telling that Paul never once uses the Greek equivalent of the term Christian when he talks about believers. Over and over again he talks about those who are "in Christ" by which he means not only

that we are members of the body of Christ, the body of believers, but also that in some sense we are "in Him." This is not the same thing as saying Christ is in you, the hope of glory, though once Paul does also say that. What is Paul talking about? He is referring to how we are being conformed to the image of Christ, now internally our mind, heart, will, emotions are being renewed day by day (see 2 Cor. 4) and one day we will be conformed to His resurrected form when Christ returns. Then we will be fully conformed to Christ's image.

The Scripture cited for the second lesson reminds us that Christians have been given right standing with God, and therefore are not in a position of being a condemned sinner, but even more importantly the Holy Spirit has set us free for the bondage the ruling principle of sin and death in our lives. Both our position and our condition has been changed as a result of Christ's death, resurrection and the internal work of the Spirit in our lives. Yet how often does it happen that Christians spend their lives feeling guilty and condemned? How often do they not really believe that they have been set free from the bondage to sin and sinful inclinations and so rationalize their ongoing bad behavior? Human beings have an infinite capacity for self-justification, and sadly many Christians do as well.

The story of John Newton is told powerfully in the movie *Amazing Grace*. Newton had been a slave ship owner and a slave trader before he was marooned somewhere and had to be rescued, an event that changed his life. He credited Christ for saving him in spite of all his horrible previous activities in enslaving other human beings. He understood that he was not saved because of his previous conduct, he was saved in spite of it! Grace by definition is undeserved benefit or blessing, and Newton knew to his very core that he was saved by amazing grace, and is credited with writing that incredibly popular hymn. Newton became a clergy person and late in life, like John Wesley, he supported young William Wilberforce who was working hard to get slavery abolished through legislation in Parliament. One of the most powerful scenes in his life is when he said to Wilberforce, "These two things I know for sure. I have been a great sinner, and Christ is a great savior." Do you also know this?

Do you know that Christ through the Spirit can set you free from the things that bewitch, bother, and bewilder you? Take time to read Rom. 8.1-4 carefully and apply it to your own life.

Thirty-fifth Sunday of the Year

"Take heed therefore to yourselves and to all the flock that the Holy Spirit has made you overseers of—feed the church of God, which he has purchased with his own blood." —Acts 20.28

Not long ago three men of eminence set forth their views of the subject of church going. These views are interesting if only because they are so widely different. The author of *The Return to Religion* says he goes to church because it is good for a person to do what he doesn't like. The second writer says, in a magazine article, that he stays away from church because the church has nothing vital, gripping, or enlightening to say. He feels like the teaching of Jesus was given too long ago. This writer fails to grasp the elementary facts of true religion. It is and must be timeless. If he had more imagination he would find every church spire gripping, the reading of the Book of books enlightening. Moreover, he is hardly in a position to improve the church whose deficiencies he laments, if he is withdrawn from all contact with it.

The third writer goes to church and unlike the first one, he enjoys going to church, it is not a necessary burden, it is a blessing, and he gets a lot out of it. He says he gets perspective, reverence, and encouragement in goodness. Almost all reasons or excuses for staying away from church resolve themselves into these three—some people have little affinity for religion, some dislike putting themselves in the way of a moral overhauling, many are misled by the idea of getting something for nothing. But by and large we get what we bring with us to church. 999 out of every 1,000 non-churchgoers would say, "I know and I want the will of Jesus to prevail in my life," and yet they stay away from the very institution whereby Jesus might prevail in their lives—the church of the living God. The will of God will be done when Christians love and live as God would have them love and live.

6/23/68

"A new commandment I give to you, that you love one another, as I have loved you." —John 13.34

The most important words are recorded in the New Testament. Everything conspires to make them impressive. They come from the lips of the world's greatest religious teacher. The occasion was the last night of His earthly life. The language suggests parental tenderness, for he calls these men "little children." It was a new commandment in its meaning. A writer says that John in his extreme old age, being carried into the church in Ephesus, was wont to repeat again and again, "Little children, love one another." When asked why he said this so many times, his reply was "It is the Lord's commandment, and if it only be fulfilled, it is enough."

It is noteworthy that the man who came nearest to the heart of Jesus came to feel that the new commandment was Jesus' crowning words. It was a new commandment in its motive. A new statement of love was now set up, *loving after the manner of Jesus Himself.* Loving the neighbor after the fashion of the Good Samaritan, or the love commanded in the golden rule is not enough. We are to love one another in that higher sense after the fashion of the Son of God. To thus love another, we must know each other better. Many Christians do not know each other, and what is worse, they do not want to know one another. Yet this was our Lord's deepest desire—to know and love each other. Has not the time arrived for believers in Jesus Christ to take Him at His word? We must if we are to inherit everlasting life. What will be your choice?

Questions and Thoughts for Reflection

1. One of the more popular bumper stickers I have seen of late proclaims, "I'm not religious, just spiritual," or words to that effect. I take it that they mean they don't go in for organized religious but

nonetheless are spiritual persons. The lesson for today reflects that sort of disaffection for the church in particular and organized religion in general in whatever form. What the bumper sticker does not say, but clearly implies is that human beings created in the image of God can't help but be religious in some way and in some sense—call it spiritual or something else. Usually, the alternative to good religion is not no religion but rather bad and inadequate religion. And yes, with all its flaws and foibles there is of course much to complain about when it comes to the church of Christ and the way it operates. The church is not just made up of Christ, it is also made up of flawed human beings, like any other organization. Or as one person put it, the church is not a museum for saints, it is a hospital for sick sinners. All are welcome to come as they are, but none of us should expect to stay as we are when we gather as the church. Christ intends to change us all into something more nearly like His image. We should all be wearing signs saying "Please be patient with me, Christian under Construction."

And yet sadly some Christians come across to non-Christians as holier than thou in all the wrong ways—exclusive rather than inclusive in mentality, judgmental of others rather than honest about their own shortcomings, clannish and sectarian rather than welcoming newcomers and strangers. Even a cursory reading of the Gospels shows Jesus banqueting with the bad, with notorious sinners, and even with the ancient equivalent of IRS agents. In His parable of the Pharisee and the tax collector he highlights a pious person who is genuinely thankful he is not like the sinful and corrupt tax collector. And yet it is the tax collector who pleads for mercy and goes away justified. Are we as church goers more like that Pharisee or more like that tax collector? Have we asked why so many people are not interested in attending our church?

2. The love Jesus is talking about in the new commandment is love between believers, and he holds his followers to a higher standard with each other than he does when he talks about his disciples loving neighbors 'as you love yourself.' Here he says we should love one another as CHRIST himself has loved us—a very high calling indeed, and what Christian is sufficient for such a love?

But perhaps we are forgetting to think about this as St. Augustine did who prayed—"give what you command Lord, and then command whatsoever you will." In short, Jesus has already made clear He is pouring His own love into us, and it's just a matter of us being a conduit of it to our fellow believers. Even outsiders noticed how deeply Jesus loved His disciples, for instance the Beloved Disciple. Remember what John 11 says that the observers said when they saw Jesus shed tears at the grave of His dearest friend? And these observers were Jewish officials, not followers of Jesus. They said "See how He loved Him." It is both a tragedy and a travesty when Christians fail to love one another following this new commandment, or worse actually, despise one another. What a terrible witness that is to the church and the world. Think on these things.

Thirty-sixth Sunday of the Year

4/7/68

"I will lift up my eyes unto the hills, from whence comes my help. My help comes from the LORD who made heaven and earth."
—Psalm 121.1-2

This psalm is one of the pilgrimage psalms. The people used them when traveling up to and camping around Jerusalem, going there to attend the Feast of the Passover, or one of the other festivals. Looking up to the hills on which the holy city was situated, they recognized the presence and blessing of God. The passage contains three suggestions.

Firstly, a high resolve—"I WILL lift up my eyes unto the hills." In the midst of disturbing circumstances, the Psalmist felt an overpowering sense of need. Instead of dwelling too much upon disappointments, one should look up to the hills where strength and happiness are to be found.

Secondly, a universal question—Where does my help come from? A question mark seems clearly to belong at the end of this sentence. It is the perpetual question of humanity and in distress: "Where shall I find help and relief, work, food, clothing, social security? Where shall I find rest for my soul, who is able to forgive me and save me?"

Thirdly, an absolute assurance—"My help comes from the LORD who made heaven and earth." If there is a God who can create all of heaven and earth, then there is reason for good confidence that He can help us in our human dilemmas.

Are you looking up to the hills in your quest for everlasting life? Only you and your Savior can know the answer. What is your decision for the future? What are you writing in your book of life?

7/11/68

"I am the Alpha and the Omega, the Beginning and the End."
—Revelation 22.16

It is disturbing to hear it claimed that God is dead and that God, heaven, and hell only find their existence within us, within the minds of human beings. The very foundations of our being are attacked by those who would ask us to agree with such a philosophy. If God is dead, do we even truly live or exist? If this is true, then our hopes, dreams and aspiration are buried with us, and like this poor mortal frame, become dust. If there is no house for us eternal in the heavens, not made with human hands, then we are condemned in finality by cruel and indomitable death. If there is nothing beyond the grave, then we cannot be with those we have loved and lost in eternity. If all this is true, then surely the struggle of this life avails nothing.

This philosophy has been soundly refuted by the historical facts that Jesus of Nazareth lived among humankind for nearly a third of a century, was crucified by a historical person, Pontius Pilate, and arose victorious over the grave, and then lived amongst His disciples for forty days proving his reality and power again and again. If the latter part of that sentence is not true, it is impossible to understand how Jesus ever had the impact He did on human history ever since then. He and His teaching and miracles should have been lost in the sands of time, His claims refuted by the most shameful way to die known in antiquity, His following stopped cold by His body moldering in the grave. Instead, a movement arose after fifty days which spread throughout the earth.

Jesus told His apostles that God the Father would fulfill His promises in a few days and baptize them with the Holy Spirit. After completing His instructions to the disciples, Jesus ascended and went to be with the Father in heaven. He had assured His followers that they too, on His return would be raised from the dead, having a resurrection body and would meet Him in the air when He returns.[1] In the meantime we should say with Micah, "And what does the LORD require of you but to do justice, to love mercy, and to walk humbly with your God" (Mic. 6.8)?

Yes, my friends, for those who reject God, based on the dim light of nature and the religion of reason there is no hope of immortality, and they know not that there bodies will go down into the earth like the beasts of the field, there to remain, decaying unto dust. But if they find this wonderful book and learn of the power of God, they will come to believe in immortality, begin to understand about resurrection. When they reach the point of full surrender to the Lord then they will know by the redeeming power of Jesus Christ that their bodies will be raised incorruptible. When we look around us in the Springtime and see the budding of the flowers and trees, we are thereby reminded that new life can happen, that we can survive the grave and bear a near resemblance to the Supreme Being, the one who makes all things live and who will never die.

Therefore, let us imitate the example of the Stranger from Galilee who is able to translate us from the imperfect to that perfect, glorious and celestial home above, where the Supreme architect of the universe presides forever.

Questions and Thoughts for Reflection

1. In the first lesson for today my grandfather reflects on the pilgrimage psalms or songs. These songs were sung by the believers as they travelled to Jerusalem going up to the festivals on Mt. Zion. These journeys did not happen as a result of a spur of the moment decision. If one was coming all the way from Galilee, it was at least a three days journey worth of walking, and one had to bring food and

---

1. At this juncture Pop seems to assume that Jesus returns at the second coming to take believers back to heaven with Him permanently, having prepared such a place, according to his reading of John 14–17. This is not a theology of the rapture; it is a belief that heaven is our final destination, though 1 Corinthians 15 and Revelation 20–22 among other texts say otherwise. In other words, he does not appear to see life in heaven as an interim condition for the believer but rather the final place we shall be. Some of his other reflections may suggest he changed his mind later.

drink and other things to camp out along the way, unless one could rely on the standing hospitality in the villages in southern Galilee and northern Judaea. As Pop says, it took a real commitment and real resolve to make a journey like that. It did not happen by accident.

Secondly, this pilgrim already knows why he is going. He is going for some help, and he knows his help comes from the one and only Lord God Almighty. He believes he can draw closer to God by going up to Jerusalem, presumably to the Temple itself where God was thought to be especially present. Thirdly, the psalmist knows that his God has already helped him and can help him. What help he needs is a very small request compared to what a God who made heaven and earth is capable of doing.

Have you ever gone on retreat, looking for an opportunity to draw closer to God, and perhaps get some help from Him? Sometimes a change of scene, and a pilgrimage somewhere can remove one's immediate concerns at home from one's sight for a time, and place oneself in a place where you can hear God's voice more clearly. Remember Elijah who traveled all the way to Mt. Sinai in order to hear God's word to him, which was not to give up on God's people, but rather the story involves a recommissioning of him and a promise of more human help for his ministry in Israel. Perhaps you need not just a recharging of your spiritual batteries but a recommissioning? Spend some time reflecting on the cited Psalm above.

2. Perhaps you've seen the billboard which quotes the German philosopher Friedrich Nietzsche saying, "God is Dead—Nietzsche." And then below it there is the retort which reads "Nietzsche is Dead—God." In those kinds of arguments usually nothing is resolved. My own experience is that often people don't think through the consequences of denying the existence of the Biblical God. They try to find some alternative way to believe in everlasting life and avoid the notion that death is the end of all persons, but alas, almost all of these suggestions are lame compared to the robust picture of the afterlife found in Revelation. Who wants to go through the spin cycle of reincarnation and come back as something less than human if you've had bad karma in life? Who wants to become some sort of ghost or

spirit who wanders the underworld but is never at rest, never a peace? I could go on. The point in part of this lesson is that you need to count the cost of rejecting the Biblical God, and worse than what I've already mentioned is punching a one-way ticket to Hell. The afterlife is not like going to a buffet in which you get to pick from various positive options. I would recommend reading C. S. Lewis's classic book *The Great Divorce* and perhaps going to see the play that is based on that book if possible. One thing is for sure: no one can afford to be wrong about the afterlife, as there are eternal consequences involved.

Thirty-seventh Sunday of the Year

2/1/81

"When the LORD brings you into the land of the Canaanites, which he swore to your fathers to give you, a land flowing with milk and honey...." —Exodus 1.3-5

One of the most dramatic confrontations in all of Scripture took place when God called Moses to lead the children of Israel out of bondage. You will recall that Moses offered excuses to God. He protested that he was not the man for the job. He exclaimed, "Who am I that I should go to Pharaoh and that I should bring the children of Israel out of Egypt?"[2] He wanted no part of what seemed an impossible situation. But God met all of Moses' arguments. At last, the servant accepted his commission, accompanied with his brother Aaron.

Moses sought an audience with Pharaoh but Pharaoh was not a man to reason with. He was hard to convince of anything. He laughed at them. He refused to take them seriously. But what no man given to pride and arrogance can ever understand is that the messengers of God are seldom deterred by men. Moses said, "Just as it is written, thus says the LORD the God of Israel—LET MY PEOPLE GO!"

---

2. This is yet another attempt at making excuses because Moses was raised in the court in Egypt and knew the situation perfectly well. He is even likely named after one of the pharaohs as his name is not a Hebrew name. Moses is probably named after the pharaoh at the time of his birth, perhaps Thutmoses II or perhaps one of the Ramses, which in Egyptian is Ra-Moses.

Throughout eleven chapters of Exodus, Moses, consecrated with the power of God slowly turned the self-satisfied sneer of Pharaoh's face into a forlorn frown. So, after four hundred years of bondage, the man who had asked God, "Who am I?" led his people out of their land of captivity. On that night a nation was born, but it would still be forty years before they would reach the promised land.

America has drifted away from God's way, as did Pharaoh. Today in our country when so much has been given to so many in the way of individual liberty, the only nation that has cherished inalienable rights, will our leaders be as foolish as Pharaoh? It sure is a question we need to ponder at this time. And yet still, with all our shortcomings, we are still by far the greatest nation on earth, a land of plenty, flowing with milk and honey. It is a matter however of whether we are on God's side, not whether He is on ours. I believe most of us are. It is after all your land and my land, and yes God's land. In God we trust. Let's keep it that way.

2/10/74

"And Moses stretched out his hand over the sea, and the LORD caused the sea to go back, by a strong east wind all that night which made the sea dry land and the waters were divided." —Exodus 14.21-30

The children of Israel passed through the Red Sea at night on dry land with a wall of water on each side of them. When the morning came and the Egyptians saw what happened they rushed into the midst of the sea. Pharaoh's chariots and men all drowned as the waters rushed together. The children of Israel were saved but the judgment was upon the Egyptians who had enslaved them. When the Israelites saw the great disaster which the Lord had brought the Egyptians they feared and believed the Lord and His servant Moses. There had to be more than human ingenuity available. Humanity's extremity is God's opportunity. God turned their problem, the barrier of the Red Sea, into the instrument of their protection.

Simon Peter was preaching God's redeeming power to both Jews and Gentiles alike. If God did not spare the angels that sinned, then surely His judgment will be visited upon all the ungodly. He did not spare the old world, but did spare Noah, so that the world might be reinhabited. It would perhaps have been better for the people not to know the way of righteousness than after having known it to turn from the commandments of the Lord delivered to them.

In 2 Peter we read that one day with the Lord is as a thousand years, and a thousand years as one day. The Bible says the Lord will come again when we least expect it, and the heavens shall pass away, the elements shall melt, and the earth shall burn up, and the righteous will be taken up in a cloud and there shall be a new heaven and a new earth, for the former things will have passed away. And there will be no more suffering, sin, or sorrow, disease decay or death, or judgment either. And God will be our God and we will be His people to live with Him in glory forever.

Questions and Thoughts for Reflection

1. I want to focus on Moses' (and God's) perseverance until the Hebrews were finally allowed to leave Egypt. Perseverance is often necessary when dealing with adamant people who do not embrace the Biblical God and His mandates.

Adoniram Judson was a missionary to Burma for many years, decades in fact, but without any converts. In fact, he spent forty years in Burma, and after the first ten years there were only eighteen converts. For the first several years there were none. He had to teach himself the Burmese language. How many of us would have had the perseverance to stick with the task in a largely Buddhist country that did not welcome the Gospel especially when it landed him in jail for a time? And yet Judson not only stuck with it, he survived imprisonment and torture for the sake of the Gospel. You can read a good summary of his ministry on Wikipedia. His ministry was almost as astounding as the ministry of Moses.

This raises the question, how persistent are we for the Lord? Or do we readily give up when things don't seem to go right or prosper? Do we say to ourselves, "Well, perhaps that was not what God wanted me to do, and just quit"? One of our major problems is that in the age of modern technology we have come to expect instant everything—instant answers, instant results, instant church growth. We are an impatient people made worse by the speed of our technology and what it can produce. But there is another dimension to this story as well.

We are told several times that Pharaoh hardened his own heart. We are also told that God at one point confirmed him in the hardness. It was not one or the other but both that led to disaster for Pharaoh's family and future. Sometimes God allows people to have the consequences of their actions, particularly if they are sinful and stubborn people. While some may think this unkind, we have to ask the question, where would we be as fallen human beings if there were not ever negative moral consequences for godless and immoral and just plain stupid actions? We would have a world of total depravity and chaos. And consequences even to simple actions seem reasonable; if I put my hands too close to an open flame, I will get burned and it will hurt. But imagine if God had made us without nerve endings in our fingers? There would be a lot of maimed human beings for sure. We have to ask the question, do we really want to live in a universe where there are not negative moral consequences to sin?

2. One of the terms you find in the Old Testament scholarly literature is redemptive judgment. This may seem like a contradiction in terms, but think for a minute about the Red Sea. The Hebrews were delivered through the Red Sea by the parting of the waters and the crossing on dry land, but those same waters which made way for the Hebrews are the very waters that drowned their pursuers and perhaps even Pharaoh himself. In the Cairo Museum there is a mummy of Rameses II, probably the Pharaoh of the Exodus. The strange thing about that mummy is that it is bright white due to high salt content. The other mummies of royalty are brownish and do not look like the mummy of Rameses II. Could it be we see evidence that he did drown in the Red Sea? It's possible.

Sometimes, redemptive-judgment involves only God's people—they are judged for their sins as part of a process of redemption. It is a regular drumbeat in the Old Testament that judgment begins with the household of God—to whom more is given more is required by God. But at no point is that sort of restorative or disciplinary judgment supposed to be the end of the story. It is supposed to lead to repentance and God's people turning back to God. The same applies to all those preliminary judgments in Rev. 6–19. At the end of each cycle there is silence, as heaven waits to hear the prayers of repentance. It is a mistake to assume that God would not judge or discipline us. Indeed, it could even be said that God chastens the most those He loves the most. Flabby Christianity too often assumes a sort of love that is not holy love, not a love that cleanses us of sin. The Bible says otherwise. When you think of God's holy love and how He disciplines those He loves, what conclusions do you draw about your own life? I once wrote a poem for Lent entitled RSVP which included the following stanza:

God's ways are not our ways,
Our eyes cannot see,
The logic of love,
Nailed to a tree.

Until we can see the logic of love nailed to a tree, we will not understand God's holy love and how He deals with our sins.

Thirty-eighth Sunday of the Year

9/8/68

"He that endures to the end shall be saved." —Matthew 10.22

The New Testament was written to comfort and establish Christians in their faith and to keep them from forgetting or forsaking their fellowship with the Lord. It is an appeal to human beings at war with evil, which was going on around them, helping them to stand fast. It is a cry and a warning to us who have named the holy name lest we abandon our faith or fall away. There can be no retreat in the warfare of the spirit. The soldiers of the cross must not yield. We worship the one true God no matter what the future holds. We serve Him for who and what He is, not for what we can get out of Him.

Remember the story of Shadrach, Meshach, and Abednego in Daniel? Into the fire they were cast and the king said, "Didn't we cast three into the conflagration, and yet there is a fourth in there who has the likeness of a son of the gods." God didn't save them from the fiery ordeal; He walked with them through it.

There is no retreat and certainly no promise that there won't be severe trials, difficulties dangers. What is promised is that He will walk through the fire with us. So, no retreat in prayers, our endeavors for the coming of the Kingdom on earth, and our walk becomes an endless adventure for our souls. We must ever be on our upward way. We cannot and must not turn back. Our journey ends only at the gates of the City of God. Our warfare is accomplished only when we are crowned victors in the spiritual city.

To each one who has named the name of Christ, each one who has heard the call to discipleship and service, who has been summoned to the holy life comes the same warning against falling away, the same call to endure to the end, but with it comes the same promise of sustaining power and sustaining grace. Christ didn't promise that God would give us all things. He did promise to give always the companionship and help of the Holy Spirit. That is worth more than anything else.

The fiery trial comes to all, in the form of sickness, disillusionment, misunderstanding, persecution, loneliness, defeat, and death. Everyone is tempted to cry 'God is able to deliver but why doesn't he? Doesn't He care? Yes, He cares. He gave His Son on Calvary that all might have everlasting life. All that He requires is for us to have faith so that we may find the comfort and strength of companionship with God. This is the victory. Then He once more asks, "Will you also go away?" And with Peter we reply, "To whom shall we go? You have the words of eternal life."

8/1/71

"That in the age to come he might show the exceeding riches of his grace in his kindness towards us through Jesus Christ." —Ephesians 2.7

The impelling urgency of any creator is self-expression. This is also true with the acts of God. He does things for His name's sake, so that He might show the exceeding riches of His grace. What then is grace? Not only the greatest word in the Bible, it is also the greatest conception that ever dawned on the mind of a human being. It is a heavenly thing, and in the sense used here it is found only in the New Testament. It must be distinguished from the power of God, the holiness of God, from His wisdom, from His justice. These of course may be witnessed, but grace is experienced. It also must be distinguished from the love of God. Grace is greater than love. It is grace which in the ages to come the Lord purposes to demonstrate to all the created universe. How? Human beings are to be kind to each other because they are brothers and sisters. Maybe that is why God is bound to be kind to human beings, because He is their Father.

The experience of grace is a present possession, but that is not all. The purpose of God contemplates the ages to come, when before principalities and powers His grace is to be demonstrated. All this is Christ Jesus. Then shall be given Him a name which is above all names. Then shall every knee bow and every tongue confess He is Lord to the glory of God the Father. The very purpose of creation, the ultimate purpose of God is to save us through grace, God's unearned, undeserved, unmerited grace.

Questions and Thoughts for Reflection

1. There has developed in America, and elsewhere a sort of false theology of faith. If you only have enough faith you won't have to suffer, it suggests. If you only have enough faith, you won't have to go through fiery trials, or cancer, or car wrecks, or the loss of a child and the list goes on and on. But if a person even spends a little time studying the history of Christianity you can quickly figure out this is bogus theology. Read Hebrews 11—those who are listed in the hall of faith had every imaginable kind of suffering and some were martyred. In fact, the more faithful you are, the more likely you are to suffer for your faith in many countries.

In the lesson for today there is a discussion of Shadrach, Meshach, and Abednego. God did not rescue them from the fiery ordeal, His representative walked with them through it, protecting them. My grandfather is right; God promises to be with us through all the trials and temptations we face. He does not promise we will be immune from or not have to have such experiences. Indeed, various passages suggest that such experiences actually can strengthen one's faith. As Jesus says, in this world we have trouble, but He has overcome this world, even overcoming death. Jesus Himself suffered many things and died a martyr's death, and it wasn't because He lacked enough faith. By no means. So it's time for us to stop beating ourselves up when something bad happens to us, thinking it was due to a lack of faith. In most cases, that is not true.

The other side of this coin is that how we approach difficult circumstances is crucial. Greater is He who is in us than anything the world can throw at us, and Romans 8 promises that no external forces or circumstances or persons can separate us from the love of God in Christ. This does not mean that you yourself can't commit apostasy. However unlikely, it can be done. Let me be clear that the Bible doesn't teach you can lose your faith like you might lose a pair of glasses. Apostasy doesn't happen by accident. It is a willful wrenching yourself free from the firm grasp God has on your life. This is why Jesus exhorts us that we must be faithful to the end. It is interesting that in Revelation those who are said to overcome are those who are faithful even unto a martyr's death. Victory, paradoxically enough, involves apparent defeat as one dies for what one believes. Victory involves not committing apostasy and not allowing any human circumstance to cause you to waver or abandon your faith even if you must suffer and die for it. Ask yourself this question: Is my concept of victory like that in Revelation? Does my concept of faith include faithfulness even unto death, even if it involves a great deal of suffering? Many of the ideas some Christians take for granted, for the Gospel, about faith and faithfulness simply aren't true. Think about these things.

2. The lesson on grace is an important one. The two things my grandfather lauds the most in these lessons is love and grace, and here he says grace is the greatest thing of all—God's undeserved, unmerited, free grace. He emphasizes that grace is something experienced. It is not merely an abstract concept or idea. Grace does things. It changes people. Interestingly, he associates it with our being kind to each other. What is your understanding of grace? How does it differ from God's love? What does it really mean to be gracious and kind to other human beings in general and believers in particular?

Thirty-ninth Sunday of the Year

5/26/68

"I bear in my body the marks of the Lord Jesus." —Galatians 6.17

Why do we experience trouble, pain, sickness, sorrow and all the rest of our trials? Why does God permit adversity to exist? This is an age-old problem and seems insoluble. But there are some platitudes that we often forget: 1) God permits these things to remind us we are still in the wilderness and not as yet, at home. When things go well with us, we are constrained to forget God and scorn the promised land. Many a person turns his back on the church, never opens the Bible, seldom prays, and is blind to the spiritual interpretation of life until he loses his money or God allows a yawning grave to open at his feet; 2) Trouble is the stamp upon all God's coinage, the mark of the King upon all His subjects. Without trouble we are none of his; 3) Trouble is calculated to bring out the best that is in us. The best or the worst, that depends on us, on how we respond to it. But the beneficial ministry of trouble is inherent in the heart of disorder; 4) Trouble opens the sluice gates of sympathy. It is good for us to have been in trouble, for then we really sympathize with other people in their afflictions. As the prophet said, "I sat where they sat." That makes all the difference. To be at one with those who have passed through the dark tunnel, you must have passed through the dark tunnel yourself. The sorrowing whom you seek to comfort know—yes, they always know—when you have also had such an experience, when you too bear the marks of Jesus Christ our Lord. You will know as you are known, never more to walk alone.

3/24/74

"For my people have committed two evils—they have forsaken me, the fountain of living waters, and hewed themselves out their own cisterns that can hold no water." — Jeremiah 2.13

Human beings need something more substantial and lasting than material things. They need God, the source of every good and perfect gift. How tragic it is for a person living in a hill country to forsake a fountain of fresh spring water in order to dig out a cistern, and then find out it can hold no water. People have been trying to do without God and to find satisfaction in material things alone, things that finally cannot fully satisfy.

Not long ago a leader in India after having lived an active life, but evidently without God, uttered this cry of despair, "Oh what am I to do? I am miserable, lonely and unhappy. Yet I cling to my miserableness. But I do want to get rid of it, but I don't know how."

The parable of the prodigal son shows us that he was miserable and unhappy, but when he realized his plight, he thought of his father and home. So, he came back to his father but not before he had spent all his inheritance and had even eaten seedpods with the pigs! Finally, he realized how wrong he had been and was returning home to ask for forgiveness so that he might work for his father as a servant. His father would not hear of this, and everything was changed for him.

Why should we labor for that which does not satisfy us? The things on which we rely to the exclusion of God do not permanently satisfy us nor are they dependable. Israel depended on Egypt, especially during a famine, and on Syria too and not upon God, and they were ashamed of both because they did not prosper with either association.

God calls us to return to Him. Shall we not listen to His voice? "Behold, I stand at the door and knock." The decision is in our hands. If we obey, we shall have wonderful peace and joy and fellowship with Him. Open the door and let Him in.

Questions and Thoughts for Reflection

1. "Man is born for trouble as the sparks fly up," says the Old Testament. Trouble of course is almost always viewed negatively. It is interesting that Representative John Lewis who was a civil rights leader before he served in Congress spoke of "good trouble." He was a Christian person who even forgave a white man who came to his office in D.C. confessed that he had beaten him during the civil rights march with Dr. King (see the movie *Selma*) and asked for forgiveness. And John gave it to him. Frankly, that's not natural, that's supernatural.

My grandfather points out that trouble is used by God to shape our character in positive ways. God also allows trouble to remind us that we have not yet arrived at our eternal destination and so we need to keep pressing on even through trouble. Trouble can bring out the best in us. Think for example of all the profiles in courage that emerge from war situations or during the pandemic caused by COVID-19, or those who have courageously battled cancer and won the battle, and are better persons for it. God does not send us trouble, but in His hands it can be used for good in our lives. What sorts of good trouble have you faced in your life? Have you ever stood up against injustice of some sort? How about unfairness and inequity in the work place? Have you ever been able to be courageous enough to witness for Christ in a volatile situation?

2. If you want to discuss an exercise in futility think for a minute of someone trying to make bricks without clay, or cement without proper gravel, or to make lemonade without a single lemon! Our text in the second lesson has God complaining that He has already provided His people with springs of living water, and instead they have chosen to try and dig their own cisterns. They didn't want to be beholden to God, or anyone else. Desiring not to be a sycophant, or lazily depend on others for things you are equipped to do for yourself is one thing. Refusing to receive the blessings that only God can give you is another. It is quite impossible for a human being to ever outgrow a need for God. We were made for relationship with God and we will always be His creatures, whether we want it or like or

not. He will always care for and love us, whether we respond or not. But human pride of the sort that says, "Thank you, God, but I can do that for myself," when you can't is absurd. That sort of pride is one of the seven deadly sins. There is a fine line between being dependably self-starting, and being self-serving and assuming you can entirely take care of yourself. Our relationship with God is not an example of codependency. God is also not a crutch to prop us up when we need it. God is our Father, and He can do for us what no one else can. He is our constant support and providential caretaker and companion through life. What experiences have you had in life that reminded you that you are not entirely self-sufficient as a human being? In what way has your pride gotten in the way of your relationship with God from time to time?

Fortieth Sunday of the Year

9/5/71

"Stir up the gift of God which is in you, for God has not given us a spirit of fear but of power and of love, and of a sound mind."
—2 Timothy 1.6-7

These words were addressed to Timothy by Paul. Timothy had been active in preaching the Gospel and possibly was showing signs of discouragement. And Paul, caring deeply and deeply interested in this young man whom he called his spiritual son, felt that Timothy needed a little stirring. So Paul did the stirring. A young Christian man was stirred to greater activity by an older and more experienced preacher. How different the world would be today, what progress would be made in its evangelization if professed Christians might be stirred to greater use of their gifts.

And we all have such gifts, because God gave them to us, and He rightly expects that these gifts should be used by each of us. Yet so many Christians who are also professed followers of Christ are making very slight use of these gifts from above, or are neglecting them altogether. Oh, that we all should get busy! There is so much to be done, souls to be directed, troubled people to be comforted, the down and outs to be lifted up and brought in. And yes, we have the gifts to do these very things. God is mindful of everybody and so often would work with and through us, just to get busy, and stop berating our own abilities to avoid responsibilities. We need to cease comparing our gifts to that of others, and instead use and use fully the gifts that are ours. How different the world would be if we did this. Even if we don't have the leverage to move the world, we can at least do some moving of those things that are near at hand. We should pray earnestly that God helps us to do just that.

2/23/69

"Behold I stand at the door and knock. If any one hears my voice and opens the door, I will come into him and will sup with him and he with me." —Revelation 3.20

One of the great needs of the Christian life is time, time for the building up of ourselves in a remembered consciousness of God. We live busy lives and have little leisure time, if by that we mean time for meditation and reflection, true leisure for the soul to recollect. God can be found in any minute during the course of the day. Prayer opens the door of our life to the entrance of His spirit.

On a holiday at noon the manager of an office told his office workers they could have the rest of the day off. In a few minutes he saw one girl still sitting at her desk, so he said, "You may go now." She answered, "I will soon, but just now I am praying." Any day, and any time of day is a good time to pray. Today, for instance, is a good time to pray. There must be the power of prayer and its result in the life of every active dedicated Christian if results are to be attained in witnessing for Christ. We should be active in fighting against evil wherever we find it.

Yet we need to remember that the Jesus who cleansed the Temple and dined with tax collectors and sinners was the same Lord who spent nights in prayer upon the mountains and died with a prayer on His lips for His enemies. Many times, He was alone in prayer. He made it a point to speak to the Father alone. Do you have time to be alone with Jesus? If you have a business appointment or an appointment at the beauty parlor, or at the fishing pier or at the golf course, you keep that appointment, don't you? We should also have an appointment with God each day and be very sure to keep it. Do we allow our lives to become so crowded that the things that matter most are crowded out? We fail to find time for prayer.

There was a man who said he prayed in bed, but often fell asleep while praying, so he felt he should do something to change this. On his way to work each day he passed through a park so he made up his mind to pray each time while passing through the park. It took him two or three minutes to go from one side of the park to the other. But the fact is he made a place and a time to have an appointment with God, a time to be alone with the Savior. Jesus is waiting for your call.

Questions and Thoughts for Reflection

1. Sometimes, many of us need someone to light a fire under us so we will get on with doing what God wants us to do in life. It should not take a taser or a cattle prod to get us motivated to serve God. In our first text for today, Paul exhorts Timothy to do something for himself—namely stir up the gift that he already had for ministry. Apparently, Timothy was timid, or afraid. He knew he was not Paul, but that didn't mean he could be the best Timothy possible. The threefold things Paul lists are interesting as gifts from God—the first of which is the power to do the ministry, the second of which is the love necessary to really have compassion for lost persons, and even troubled found ones. The third one is the spirit of a sound mind. Why do you think Paul mentioned this? Paul is talking about having and using sober judgment about things. Sometimes Christians have a zeal that is not according to knowledge, to use a Biblical phrase.

The story is told of a famous Knute Rockne speech given to his struggling Notre Dame football team. They were in a new locker room in a new stadium at Illinois. At the end of the speech with some vigor Knute said, "And now let's all rise as one and run through those doors and on to victory." Just one problem, on the other side of the doors he pointed to was the new natatorium and some of the first players who ran through the door fell into the swimming pool!

Zeal for the Lord, and hard work for the Lord is good, but one's efforts have to be pointed in the right direction. One has to use sound judgment to decide how to accomplish the task. It's no good picking up a Phillip's head screwdriver to screw in a flat head screw.

Have you ever taken time to evaluate what gifts God has given you? Have you been diligent to use them in His service? There are all sorts of gifts you know. Dr. John Ed Mathison used to assign some of his parishioners in Montgomery Ala. to be eagle-eyed moving van watchers. When they saw a new family moving into town, they were to take them a pie, welcome them to town and invite them to come to church. This resulted in many new members! On the other hand, there are people who think they have a gift from God, and they have mis-evaluated the situation. Some people think they can sing, when they really don't have that gift. Discernment is the key here, and being evaluated by others that know what the various gifts look like and amount to. Have you ever taken an inventory that evaluates your spiritual gifts? There are such tools, and we all should avail ourselves of them.

2. Our second lesson is about making regular appointments to talk with God. My grandfather is right to urge us to do this, otherwise the tyranny of the urgent crowds out our prayer time, or we leave it to the end of the day, when we say our night prayers to God that sometimes quickly turn into silent prayers as we fall asleep too quickly. I like the story about the man who decided he would pray his way through the park on the way to work. It is always possible to carve out some time for God if you are willing. This is important for a variety of reasons. Communication is a means of communing, of loving God, of showing you love Him regularly. Even if you are not good at praying public prayers, this should not affect your private conversations with God. I would urge don't wait until you have a problem to talk to God. Think about God as your friend and confidant, and talk to Him about anything you might talk to your spouse, or your best friend, or your parents about. Do you have a regular prayer practice? Is it at a set time each day, or does it vary? Make a point to make regular appointments with God. His line is always open, and he's always there.

Forty-first Sunday of the Year

1/3/74

"For our light and momentary afflictions worked for us a far more exceeding and eternal weight of glory. So, we look not to the things which are seen but to the things which are not things. For the things that are seen are temporal, but the things which are not seen are eternal." —2 Corinthians 4.17-18

We are living in the midst of a troubled world, without a doubt. It has been jarred loose from its old moorings and certainties. A great cloud of confusion, of anxiety and fear rests heavily over all peoples. But in the words cited above the earnest, believing Christian finds comfort and strength. Paul's design is to show the sources of consolation, strength, courage, support in times of trial and testing. We do not welcome afflictions, but it is true that under the marvelous providence of our heavenly Father, they do work for us an eternal weight of glory, or character. What a comfort for the Christian to know that behind the dim unknown stands God within the shadows, keeping watch above His own. The things which are seen are those created things of which we have knowledge through the senses and which pass away. The things which are unseen are the things of the spirit, moral principles, truth and God, and these must be apprehended or perceived by the eye of faith. They are our greatest forces abiding forever in the moral universe. These are real and mighty. A man dying cried out, "My friends, these are real and are mighty." God, Christ, eternal life, heaven, the glory these are the great realities. Though they are unseen they are the comfort of believing Christians. For here we catch the vision of God's gracious purpose, eternal glory and eternal life.

The reason Paul speaks of the "weight of glory" is he is envisioning a scales. He says in one pan in the scales there are things temporal and temporary, things seen about which we can say "this too will pass." All our trials and tribulations are in that pan in the scale. But in the other pan are things that are eternal, not temporary, and are unseen—things like love, grace, and of course God. When you weigh these things in the balance, the scales always tip to the side where the eternal weight of glory is. Always. In this we should take comfort.

8/8/71

"Jesus went about doing good." —Acts 10.38

These seven words from one verse constitute a biography of our Lord in miniature. Jesus, the only begotten Son of His Father, the Messiah, and later the risen Lord was content during His stay upon this earth to go about doing good. Nazareth was a small and lowly place. This fact encourages us in the knowledge that no matter what our circumstances in life we may aspire to follow in the Master's footsteps. Jesus "went," so many are content with the intention of going! "I meant to go," they say. "He went about." He did not wait for some call from a faraway place. He found great need right at His doorstep and He began there.

What a busy little word is "do." It emphasizes energy, definite action and achievement. It's meaning is positive and constructive. It could even mean accomplishing. This busy energetic word conveys inspiration and encouragement. Would you forget your troubles, renew your hopes and ambitions, and find happiness? Then do as the Lord did—go about doing good for those in need, whatever the need may be. Help those who have need of help. Mere activity, whether physical or mental does not necessarily bring happiness. "Jesus went about doing good." Doing is one thing, doing good is another. Would you follow Him? Then you should follow His example and do likewise.

There are so many who are pious and whom seem content in their piety. So many pray, hope and aspire that sinners be saved, that the sorrowful be comforted, and that the troubled and lonely and discouraged find peace. Such prayers, hopes, and aspirations are worthwhile, but how pitifully empty they are without action! No matter how insignificant we may feel, no matter where we are, or what our circumstances may be, we can go about doing good for the Master and for the good of humankind.

Questions and Thoughts for Reflection

1. 2 Corinthians 4 was a favorite passage for my grandfather and for me as well. In his lesson on a portion of that chapter he does not deal with "outwardly we are wasting away but inwardly we are being renewed day after day," but it is an important context for understanding what he does say. The weak chink in the Christian's armor is the body, the part that is wasting away. The renewal we experience now is of our inner self, not our outer self. No wonder then that the sins of the flesh are what even Christians are prone to. The body is not yet made new.

Pop is right to emphasize that the 2 Cor. 4 passage is all about perspective, contrasting the temporal and temporary with the eternal. There is an interesting play on words because the word glory, doxa, in the Hebrew at least is *kavoth* and it actually means heavy, weighty. When the Psalmist asks, "Who is the King of Glory?" he is asking who is the heavy or weighty or most significant king. Thus, the phrase weight of glory is almost redundant—the weight of the weighty presence of God. Paul is urging us to weigh that weight against all things temporal and temporary, and realize that "the eternal weight of glory" outweighs anything temporal—any trial, tribulation, suffering, even death. All that is temporary is put in the shade by the permanent and lasting things—God, everlasting life, and more.

The question this lesson raises for us is how much and how often do we remember to view life with the eye of faith, with our spiritual eye on the unseen? This sort of talk may seem odd but think of what Jesus says in John 3—he says the Spirit, like the wind is unseen, but you can recognize His presence by His effects, just as you can see the effects of a strong wind by the blowing leaves or the broken tree limbs. Then too, when God does a work in a human life, when His truth takes hold there, you can see the effects on that person's character and behavior. Remember the story of Zacchaeus? Notice how his behavior as a tax collector changes when he encounters Christ? While you cannot see love, you can certainly see it in action in the warm embrace of a child, or the kiss of a spouse, and in other ways. It is true—the invisible things are the most important ones. Can you list the fruit of the Spirit, all of which are not visible things, though their effects are visible? Hate as well is not a visible thing, but oh my how very visible are its effects—consider the Nazi concentration camps.

2. Doing good. Some Christians have been beguiled into think that our doing, our works, our behavior has nothing to do with our salvation. And they are wrong. We are supposed to work out our salvation with fear and trembling as God works in us to will and to DO! Or as James says, "Faith without works is dead." Faith without works won't work, as that is not living faith. I have written a poem about this very matter which I will share here:

IF ONLY

I

I would have dressed up,
Only it was too much trouble.

I would have gone out,
Only it cost too much.

I would have driven,
Only travel's dangerous.

I would have eaten,
Only I weigh too much.

I would have danced,
Only I didn't have a partner.

I would have returned,
Only it brought back bad memories.

II

I would have gone,
Only I didn't have time.

I would have visited,
Only I wasn't wanted.

I would have tried,
Only it was a waste of energy.

I would have helped,
Only they didn't need me.

I would have cared,
Only I didn't feel like it.

I would have cried,
Only I wasn't sorry.

III

I would have volunteered,
Only I had better things to do.

I would have voted,
Only it wouldn't have changed things.

I would have donated,
Only they'd made their quota.

I would have spoken up,
Only I was afraid to.

I would have acted,
Only others got there first.

I would have felt sorry,
Only I didn't feel guilty.

IV

I would have prepared,
Only it was too much work.

I would have studied,
Only I wouldn't have passed.

I would have corrected it,
Only it was too late.

I would have told the truth,
Only it would have offended.

I would have graduated,
Only life intervened.

I would have gotten the job,
Only they didn't like me.

V

I would have prayed,
Only God already knows.

I would have worshipped,
Only I hate to sing.

I would have fellowshipped
Only I didn't know them.

I would have served,
Only I didn't have the calling.

I would have loved,
Only it hurt too much.

I would have lived,
If only.

The person just described is the very one critiqued in the lesson for today. It stands in contrast to "Jesus went about doing good." The question remains, are we just standing on the side of the road cheering Him on, or are we also "doers of the Word," doers of good as He was?

Forty-second Sunday of the Year

7/21/74

"God said: 'Come, I will send you to Pharaoh that you may bring forth my people, the sons of Israel out of Egypt . . . . I will be with you.' But Moses said, 'Who am I that I should go to Pharaoh and bring the sons of Egypt out?'" —Exodus 3.10-11

It has often been said that the world has yet to see what God can do through a man who is wholly yielded to the divine will. In a real sense, such a man once existed, and his name was Moses. After eighty years of frustration and disappointed hope, during which Moses lived the lifestyle of a fugitive from justice, he met with God in the desert and his life was changed. Moses returned to Egypt as God's messenger and agent and boldly confronted the monarch of the most powerful kingdom on earth. By the power of God, Moses compelled Pharaoh to release a displaced captive population of two million persons.[3] Then Moses led this timid and easily discouraged group of ex-slaves through the parted waters of the Red Sea and into the wilderness. Then after forty years these same slaves had been transformed into a disciplined army of warriors, able to smash the opposition of seven powerful and well-armed nations. What leader in all of recorded history can match such an achievement as this? But, of

---

3. The word in Hebrew *'lp* can mean thousand, but it can also mean group (in this case tent group). Obviously, there is a big difference between 2 million people and something like 20,000 tent groups or clans for a maximum of about 75,000 people.

course, this enormous feat was not accomplished my Moses himself, but by the grace and power of the Almighty God.

After God had called Moses' attention to the burning bush that resisted destruction by flames, he then commissioned him to lead Israel out of bondage in Egypt. Moses still felt he was inadequate for the task, and made excuses.[4] God assured him that He would be with him, so it was Moses' part to believe God's promises completely and to obey God's directions with courage and faith, and God would do the rest. God said, "Just tell them that I AM sent you," which indicated that the true and living God stood in personal relationship with His covenant people. Thus, God revealed Himself as a living being, a person who met and talked with real human beings and claimed them as His own. We see in this narrative His great love for humanity and His desire to have close relationships with human beings.

2/16/75

"At midnight Paul and Silas prayed and sang praises unto God and the prisoners heard them. Suddenly, there was a great earthquake so the foundations of the prison were shaken. And immediately all the doors were open and everyone's hands were loosed." —Acts 16.25

When out of doors, on a beautiful day walking along a flower bordered path almost anyone might be prompted to sing. At midnight in prison, with feet in shackles after a beating, well that is a different matter. Yet that night the old jail at Philippi had the surprise of its long and dreary history. Curses, groans, and wailing it had heard aplenty, no doubt. Its drab walls were covered with inscriptions of the sobs and maledictions of the years. Now there was something new and different as Paul and Silas joined that gallant company who have thrilled the world with their songs. Only those who have in their souls certain mighty convictions and beliefs can raise a song in the dark, and under such dark circumstances. If we are to keep singing in this midnight of a world we live in we must rekindle our

---

4. We know these were excuses for other texts tell us that he could speak quite well. Acts 7.22 says, "Moses was educated in all the wisdom of the Egyptians and was powerful in speech and action."

faith in humanity, and in the final triumph of right or justice. In a friendly universe with someone we can call Father at the center of it, such are the well-founded hopes we can have which enable us to keep the music going even in the darkness. Those who hold such rock-solid convictions as Paul and Silas cannot be deterred or confounded. Either during their lives or after their passing their great aims and desires come to fruition.

Paul and Silas were released and their influence has gone out to the ends of the earth. With these sorts of convictions Martin Luther played his mighty part in the Reformation, and Robert Lewis Stevenson laughed at death saying, "I believe in the ultimate decency of things." With these convictions Jesus faced a world of indifference or even hate, and endured the cross, despising the shame, and went on to resurrection morning. Do you have such a rock-solid set of convictions?

Questions and Thoughts for Reflection

1. One of the things we should appreciate about the Bible is its honesty, even about the ones we call heroes, such as Moses. The portrait of Moses in Exodus and the following books is of a man we can relate to. Sometimes he serves God well and does what God tells him to do. Sometimes, not so much, and he ends up not being allow to enter the promised land. This ending must have been profoundly disappointing after all Moses went through over various decades to get God's people to the doorstep of the promised land. I was at Mt. Nebo this past year, and the view from there of the Dead Sea, and various parts of Israel is spectacular if you can be there on a day when things are not too hazy. Moses must have thought, "So close, and yet so far away."

It had been a long journey for Moses. His name is not a Hebrew name, indeed he is probably named after the Pharaoh when he was born—Tutmoses, or less like one of the Ra-meses. He was raised in the court and well educated there as well. He was placed over various projects, including over his own people. He fled the land after murdering an Egyptian who was mistreating some Hebrew workers. He lived in peace but in obscurity starting a whole new life in Midian where he married, spent 40 years, and could not have seen coming what was next—God speaking to him in a burning bush. Reluctantly he accepts his call from God and does what he was commissioned to do. In some ways this story is like that of C.S. Lewis who when he gave in to God one day in Oxford says he was the most reluctant convert in all of Christendom.

We tend to idolize our Biblical heroes but the honesty of the account about Moses is actually helpful because it means, if God can use a reluctant figure like Moses, even when he makes some mistakes, then He can use us as well. Now one might say, "Yes, but if God doesn't work with flawed human beings, He has no humans to work with, other than Jesus of course." True, but it only took one perfect human being to bring salvation into the world, God's own Son. The ministry work before and after him could be done by people like you and me, sinners saved by God's grace.

Take some time to reflect on the story of Moses and ask yourself some serious questions. For instance, ask what excuses you have been making to not serve the Lord, or at least not fully engage in the ministry God wants you to do. Have you been using your shortcomings as an excuse to not fully engage in church, not fully use your gifts for the Lord, not take the time required to seriously study God's Word? Whatever your excuses, you are not excused. God can write straight with a crooked stick. He can use you and me. As one person said, God is mainly looking for availability not for special ability. If God was looking for 'a few good men' or women, then Jesus didn't get the memo when He picked the twelve—four fishermen, two tax collectors, two zealots, and four others. They often looked more like the dirty dozen than the magnificent Twelve—and some of their behavior and response to Jesus' teachings made them look like the DUH-sciples. They didn't get it. You get the point. If God can use Moses, if Jesus can use the Twelve, then we have no *legitimate* excuses not to hear His call on our lives and serve Him. None whatsoever.

2. Singing while in shackles in a jail. What a picture that is of Paul and Barnabas. When God intervened in Saul's life on Damascus Road one suspects that he could not even remotely imagine what would

follow that intervention. Certainly, as a Roman citizen he could not have imagined ending up in a Roman jail in remote Philippi far from his own land of Cilicia or his home since youth in Jerusalem. We should not mistake the singing of these apostles as a sort of whistling in the dark or spitting into the wind. No, it reflects their remarkable belief, confidence, trust in the Lord. My grandfather has it right when he says, "Only those who have in their souls certain mighty convictions and beliefs can raise a song in the dark, and under such dark circumstances." Their convictions were rock-solid, even in jail.

What about us? If we were put in some of the situations Paul went through in life, would our faith remain unshaken? If we were tested in as many ways and times as Paul was, would we still remain loyal to the Lord? If we asked God to remove a thorn in our flesh, clearly referring to a painful physical condition, and God said, "No—my power is made perfect in weakness, my grace is sufficient for you"—would we not protest, or be upset with God?

Take time to read 2 Cor. 11.23-28 and meditate on what it says, for this is Paul's disaster catalog:

> I have worked much harder, been in prison more frequently, been flogged more severely, and been exposed to death again and again. Five times I received from the Jews the forty lashes minus one. Three times I was beaten with rods, once I was pelted with stones, three times I was shipwrecked, I spent a night and a day in the open sea, I have been constantly on the move. I have been in danger from rivers, in danger from bandits, in danger from my fellow Jews, in danger from Gentiles; in danger in the city, in danger in the country, in danger at sea; and in danger from false believers. I have labored and toiled and have often gone without sleep; I have known hunger and thirst and have often gone without food; I have been cold and naked. Besides everything else, I face daily the pressure of my concern for all the churches.

If this leads you to shake your head and ask, how could he keep going after all that, you are forgetting about God's grace. A person doesn't know what they can go through with God's grace and a firm conviction in the Lord until the occasion occurs. You can't tell in advance. And besides, no one is asking you to do it without the strength and grace of God carrying you through it all. The question is, how much do you trust God to use you and get you through whatever situation He calls you to go through? Ask yourself—could you sing a solo, not in the choir, but in jail, knowing that God was with you?

Forty-third Sunday of the Year

1/26/74

". . . until the day that Jesus was taken up to heaven, after giving instructions through the Holy Spirit to the apostles he had chosen."
—Acts 1.2

Jesus had been giving instructions to His disciples for forty days and then He was taken up into heaven. Before this happened, He told them that while John baptized with water, they would be baptized with the Holy Spirit. They went out to preach to the people and thousands were saved, and when the day of Pentecost came, they were all with one accord in one place. What a miracle it was that those listening on that Pentecost day spoke different languages and yet they all heard the message in their own language, for the disciples had been enabled by the Holy Spirit to speak all those languages. Wouldn't it be a miracle if we could get just 100 people to completely agree at one time and in one place.

I think this passage is probably where Norman Vincent Peale got his idea to write the book *The Power of Positive Thinking*. I have read this book and it is good. In my mind, God had conditioned the minds of these men with positive thinking and gave them the mental powers to understand what was said in any language and to speak in those languages. God said He would show wonders and He really did. I think that the power of positive thinking that God bestowed on them was responsible for what happened.

A person who constantly thinks negatively will eventually imagine many things that can be harmful to themselves and those around them. Positive thinking makes a much happier outlook. Those people attending the Pentecost festival gladly received the Lord's Word and were baptized. In one day, there were three thousand added to the saved, and they continued daily with one accord wherever they went, praising God and having favor with the people.

Peter and John saw a lame man sitting at a gate asking for alms. John told him to look on us. Then Peter said 'silver and gold have I none, but such as I have I give to you. In the name of Jesus Christ rise up and walk' and he took him by the hand and the man leaped to his feet and ran praising God. Peter told the people that this was the work of God and not them. Many times we are apt to depend on ourselves and credit ourselves instead of God, but not Peter and John. They knew that they had been empowered by the Holy Spirit at Pentecost.

4/29/73

"Paul, a servant of Jesus Christ, called to be an apostle, separated for the Gospel of God . . ." —Romans 1.1

God's purpose is evident and is spelled out through the whole of Paul's letter to the Romans. Sometimes his words are as remarkable for what they suggest as for what they actually say. The Gospel of God suggests something even greater—the God of the Gospel. This is greater because apart from the living God, the Gospel itself is unthinkable. But what kind of God is He? What is His preeminent quality?

God is love. No greater thing than this can be thought or said or sung about God. All His attributes bow before the essential nature of our Father, like the sheaves of Joseph's brothers bowed before the sheaves of Joseph. Whatever else God is, the God and Father of our Lord Jesus Christ is holy love, righteous love, and absolute love. No wonder then that the Gospel of God is the very latest Good News, and will survive all other news. Much of the news today in papers or on TV is bad news about bad things happening everywhere. The context and the content are both dark. The Gospel of God is unique in this—it shines brightest in the darkest night. It rings truest in the presence of falsehood. Its justice conquers injustice. Its very loveliness transforms the unlovely. It takes the things of bad report and turns them into Christ-like excellence.

Are you fearful, lonely, hopeless, friendless, loveless? Yes, you may exclaim. Then if you are, you are just like other worldly people without the God of the Gospel and the Gospel of God. But if we are Christians having both the Gospel of God and the God of the Gospel we have all we need. We are His and He is ours, forever. Yes, we must be reconciled with God, for He alone loves us enough to offer and be able to deliver everlasting life.

Questions and Thoughts for Reflection

1. As you can see from the first lesson for today, my grandfather was duly impressed by Norman Vincent Peale's famous book. While I agree that positive thinking is an important thing for Christians to have, since the future is ultimately in God's hands and is as bright as His promises, I don't think positive thinking is what allowed those disciples to understand and speak foreign languages. I think it was a spiritual miracle, and again the miracle was not in the hearing but in the speaking. The disciples were not speaking in glossolalia and then heard in foreign languages. The Greek is clear enough—"we heard them SPEAKING in our native tongues." So the old Pentecostal interpretation of Pentecost is mistaken at this point.

Furthermore, Acts 2 is about the birthday of the church, not the second dose of the Spirit on the disciples. John 20 is about a prophetic sign act where Jesus' breathes on the disciples as a promise that the Spirit is coming on them once He ascends into heaven. And indeed, He says it is necessary for Him to leave before He can send and they can receive the Spirit. So, John 20 is not about a first installment of Spirit reception, and the proof of this is that the disciples are still behind locked doors for fear of the authorities days later when Thomas is present and Jesus reappears in the upper room. They are not out evangelizing the world between those two visits of the risen Lord to the upper room. Jesus not infrequently did prophetic sign acts such as the cleansing of the temple which was not a cleaning out of the whole temple but a sign that judgment was coming on the corruption in the temple.

I do however agree with Pop that it was a miracle that those new Christians were all of one mind and heart and in agreement at the beginning of the church. We could certainly use a miracle like that today with the church divided into hundreds of denominations, none of which fully agree with the others. It's a very poor witness to the Gospel, and very unlike the description of the church towards the end of Acts 2 and also Acts 4. Perhaps the saddest part about those accounts is that the Greek verbs can be read to mean "they used to be all in one accord." When you read Galatians 1–2 or 1 Corinthians, you realize that "accord" didn't last long.

This lesson raises profound questions for us—Why is it that Christians can't get their act together and be 'of one accord' like the beginnings of the church? Why do you think we have such deep division in the church even within individual denominations and individual churches? Are we just not listening to God and the Spirit? Think about these things.

2. The second lesson for today is another story altogether. I like my grandfather's point that the Gospel of God would be worthless, ineffective if the God of the Gospel wasn't equally real, behind it, and implementing that Good News. Just so. I have grown more than weary of ministers bragging about "how many souls I have saved." This is rather like Shakespeare's quill pen being able to speak and claim, "I wrote a lot of great plays." We are just servants of God, instruments in His hands, and we need to always keep that in mind. I have never converted anybody by my abilities or efforts. God however has used me to accomplish such things. It is Jesus who saves, not Ben. So, ministers everywhere need to take a chill pill on bragging, and more importantly a humility pill.

One of things that needs to happen for all ministers is they need to be aware of the impression and the effect they have on others. By this I don't just mean how they come across on first impressions, I mean the ongoing effect they have on their parishioners. Some ministers are just oblivious in regard to this. This is why churches need to have pastor-parish committees, or good deacons that can inform the minister of such things.

Sometimes Christians mistakenly think the Bible is magical, as if it works all on its own without God. I once had a professor who rightly said the Word without the Spirit is like dry wineskins without wine. But the Spirit without the Word is like new wine with nothing to contain it and give it shape. Both God and the Gospel are necessary for the Good News to change lives. Would you agree? What is your view on how the Gospel actually works?

Forty-fourth Sunday of the Year

5/25/75

"As Jesus said, it is more blessed to give than to receive." —Acts 20.35

When you take time to live, you begin to realize the meaning of love. Love is one of the greatest words in our vocabulary, perhaps the very greatest for God is love (1 John 4). Unselfish love is a love expressed towards others without any ulterior motive. It is a love that puts the other person first without counting the cost. The human condition is not able to create this love. Its origin and its source is the heart of God. A person can receive it from God, and then he can share it with God and His fellow human beings. The word love alone is not always sufficient since the action must go with it. Then we have loving service. This means faith, faith in God, but also faith in our fellow human beings as well. Have we begun this process in earnest? Do we love God and our neighbor? Do we have that sort of faith?

We accept the fact that love is the great unifying force in the world. We agree that everything beautiful in life is seasoned with love, but when will we begin sincerely to express to God the love we have for Him, or to our fellow human beings the love we have for them? Faith is the keystone of all Christian teaching, so we must build on our faith, on what we believe and use it to demonstrate that unselfish love is the key to getting things done. It's even the cornerstone on which to build for everlasting life. Concern for friends and others are beautiful words but what makes them beautiful is action. The best things in life are happiness, freedom, and peace of mind and are always attained by giving them to others. Yes, it is more blessed to give than to receive.

You don't know how to really live until you know how to love and not to hate. You don't know how to live until you know how to be humble and not arrogant, to forgive them that despitefully use you, or until you know how to give and not receive. You don't know how to really love until you have a daily contact with God. The secret of a happy and successful life is taking time to live and to love.

Many people have come to think that the chief virtue is to keep up with the clock, the calendar, or the Joneses. This is where life robs many of its deepest meaning and happiness. Adding years to life is important, but adding life and love to your years is much more important. We must have time for the soul, time for work, and time for others.

Life can be very great or pathetically small. It can be cheap or of real worth. It can be futile or creative. So why not take time to live the beautiful life and develop its riches before they are forever beyond reach? As the poet once said, "the saddest words of tongue or pen—what might have been, what might have been."

10/11/70

"And he gave them their request, but sent leanness into their souls."
—Psalm 106.15

When Israel lusted for meat in the wilderness, God gave them their request but also sent leanness into their souls. Physical craving was satisfied at the expense of spiritual good. Having our way is always an expensive thing. God granted Israel a king as a result of the nation's insistence, but with kings came also distress and grief and the ultimate loss of their national existence.

Jesus represented God as an indulgent father in the parable of the Prodigal Son. One half of the father's fortune was freely given to the younger son when he asked for it, which is extraordinary because normally the inheritance would only be dispensed at the death of the father. Did that young, reckless son really say or imply, "You're as good as dead, Father; give me my inheritance now"? With this gift came wandering, debauchery, hunger, and a return home in shame and disgrace. At least part of the lesson of our text is "be careful what you wish for, because what comes with it may be disastrous." Let us consider the lesson from another Psalm, Psalm 16.11 which says, "You will show me the path of life, in your presence is the fullness of joy. At your right hand there are pleasures forever more."

Believers know they are in the way of salvation, and have passed from death to life, but still, we may hanker after material things that cannot finally satisfy the deepest longings of our souls. We must reflect on the inconsistencies of our walk with God. Remember for example what Peter says in 1 Peter 3, "Whoever wants to enjoy life and have happy days must no longer speak evil, and must stop telling lies. He must turn away from evil and do good. He must seek peace and pursue it. For the Lord keeps His eye on the righteous and always listens to their prayers. But he turns against those who do evil."

One must be careful, even as a Christian, about what you pray for. If you finish your prayer with "in Jesus' name," have you ever thought that you are signing *His* name to your petition? Have you asked the question, is this something Jesus Himself would pray for? If not, then you should rethink what you are asking for. Sometimes prosperity, even if sent from God brings with it a harmful effect on the soul, encouraging covetousness among other things. Ask yourself, what would God have me do with this blessing? Think on these things.

Questions and Thoughts for Reflection

1. There is a reason why Paul, in his great love poem in 1 Corinthians 13, says, "the greatest of these things is love," even greater than faith and hope. I pondered for a long time as to why he said this. Then it dawned on me, Paul is thinking eschatologically. There will be a day when Christ returns when faith becomes sight. There will be a day when our hopes will be fulfilled and we will be able to echo Paul and say, "Who hopes for what they already have?" Love however is the one thing, the one quality, the one activity that carries on into eternity. We can do it now and later.

There is indeed a reason why the Bible says God is love, and why the first mentioned fruit of the Spirit is love, and why the greatest commandments in regard to God and neighbor and even our fellow disciples is love—we are to love God with all that we have and are, and love our neighbor as ourselves, and then there is also Jesus' final new commandment that we love our fellow believers as He has loved us. There is a reason love is a constant theme in Pop's lessons. He is making the main thing the main thing. I agree with him that you don't really know how to live until you know how to love in a godly sense of the term love. A love without ulterior motives as Pop says. But this sort of love is not natural, it comes from God Himself. If we are to share and give such love we must first freely receive it from God. There is a reason St. Augustine once said in his famous book of *Confessions*, "Give what you command Lord, and then command whatever you will." This is probably in part a result of his reflecting on John 15 and 1 John 3–5 which were so formative to Augustine's thinking about things.

Paul provides us with the cautionary warning that we can be the most gifted and talented person in our church, but without love we are a clanging cymbal, and apt to be too egotistical as well about how gifted we are. As we have said in a previous lesson, the love we are talking about can be commanded and so is *not* primarily about feelings, which cannot be commanded. It's about love in action, loving service, perhaps especially self-sacrificial service.

So, what loving service have you done recently? What loving service should you be doing even now? What does it mean to love your fellow believers like Christ loves you? Remember, the New Testament is clear (see Rom. 5) that God has first poured His own love into your hearts, so it's not a matter of you generating this love simply out of your own strength or will power or desire. It's about you becoming a channel for God's love to flow through you to others, without any requirement of payback or reciprocity. You simply give with no thought of return. Would you agree that we are most Christlike when we are least focused on self and what is in it for ourselves? Unfortunately, the consumer approach to everything has infected the church so that instead of asking what can I give, you have comments like 'I don't go to that church or that service because I don't get anything out of it.' This is the opposite of relating to one's fellow believers in love.

In my home church in Charlotte, North Carolina, there was a little old lady who was a regular and sat in the same pew each week. She had thick glasses and hearing aids, but there she was week and week. One Sunday, a young woman who sat in the same pew, being puzzled by the lady, asked her, "Ma'am, if you don't mind me asking, why are you here, since you can't get much out of the service anymore? I can see you struggling to see and struggling to hear what is said." The older woman's response was classic: "I am here not so much for what I can get out of the service but for what I come to give—I come to praise my Lord, I come to offer my prayers and tithes, I come to be with God's people and show love for them, and be a good example of faithfulness, even though I don't get as much out of the service as I used to. But the reason for coming to church is for what you can give, not what you can get."

The younger woman, caught up in the consumer mentality approach to life and even to church attendance, was shocked by this response. But the older woman was speaking the truth in love. In fact, she got news in advance each week about what Scriptures and hymns would be used in the service, and she read through them before she came to church, so she was better able to be prepared to give and also benefit from the service. Hopefully, we are all more like that little old lady in our approach, for that is the approach of Christian love.

2. There are two vital points in the second lesson for today. The first is, be careful what you ask God for, for He may give it to you. Sometimes God gives us what we request, not because He thinks it will be a blessing or necessarily good for us, but in order to teach us a lesson or to test us. God gave His people a human king, but it was not His highest wish for His people. The second equally vital point from this lesson is that once God gives you a gift, you can either use it to His glory and for human edification, but you can also abuse it and use it wrongly. I remember well going to an annual conference meeting

and hearing a truly remarkable and gifted preacher give us three powerful lessons. Only shortly thereafter we learned that his wife was found strangled with a coat-hanger in their garage, and that this minister had been carrying on an affair with the daughter of another famous clergyman in secret all the while. It turns out he was using his gifts to attract not merely attention, but also the affections of someone other than his wife. But you can see this same sort of abuse of gifts in Scripture itself. Go back and read the story of Elisha, the children and the bears in 2 Kings 2.23-25. This is a classic example of a prophet behaving badly. He didn't like being mocked by children, and so he used his spiritual power that God had given him to curse the children and in turn they were mauled by bears. Yes, we can use or abuse the gifts God gives us. Can you remember or cite example of the misuse of spiritual gifts that you have seen? What did your leaders or church do about it?

Forty-fifth Sunday of the Year

11/10/71

"Not that I speak in respect of want, for I have learned in whatsoever circumstance I am in, to be content. I know both how to be abased and how to abound. Everywhere and in all things I am instructed both to be full and to be hungry, both to abound and to suffer need. I am able [to endure] all things in Christ who strengthens me."
—Philippians 4.11-13

These words may seem impertinent to this maladjusted time. But Paul knew of even worse conditions earlier, and besides, his earlier ambitions had fitted him for contentment. Eagerness for self-advancement never does. But when Jesus put Paul to the test, he passed triumphantly.

Yet Paul's contentment mentioned in our text was not an apathetic acceptance of things as they were. Never was there a more determined fighter against the status quo than Paul. Paul's contentment rested on the fact that all of life is in God's hands—not just the good which we usually count on, but also the evil which we have to endure and overcome. Paul believed that God built a purpose into the world. God pronounced it very good. Paul therefore had only to adjust himself to the purpose that still remained and to vindicate it. Paul believed that God placed a sense of personal destiny into every human heart, a delightful one for those who believe in Him.

This provided a fruitful task that could not end in bankruptcy, rather fulfillment waited at the end of the road both for God's cosmic purposes but also for his own personal destiny. Like God's Word,

Paul believed that all his faith and efforts would not return to him void. Therefore, even in difficult times, even under house arrest he was in good spirits, knowing that 'greater is he who is in us' than anything the world can throw at us. Our God, not our circumstances controls and guides our lives. We cannot control all the things that will happen to us, but by God's grace and guidance we can control how we will respond. What we see in Philippians 4 is how Paul responded to both prosperity and adversity. Do we follow the apostle's example?

9/12/71

"Remember that Jesus Christ, the seed of David, was raised from the dead, according to my Gospel." —2 Timothy 2.18

These words were written by Paul, the many-scarred veteran of the cross, to his spiritual son, Timothy. They have a pertinent and peculiar application to us in our day. Paul the aged warrior at this time is a prisoner in Rome, facing certain death. Timothy, his first lieutenant in the Christian army is in Ephesus and has charge of all the churches in Asia Minor. Ephesus is a great world city, but it is also a pagan city housing many religions, many cults, theories, philosophies, -isms, emphases, and practices. In the face of all these conflicting and confusing philosophies and practices what is Timothy to believe and to do?

We in our day in the midst of increasingly pagan surroundings and practices are asking the very same question. What are we to believe and to do? Paul's guiding word to Timothy and to us is believe, teach, emphasize, and do whatever squares and harmonizes with the person of Jesus Christ who was both a living human being of Davidic descent raised from the dead, and also divine. What a reassuring word that is. How comforting to know that in all the involved, complicated, conflicting and confusing teachings, theories, philosophies and practices that surround us, we may be sure that whatever fits with, harmonizes and squares with, the living human and yet divine person of Christ is safe to accept, to follow, and to do. And whatever does not square up or harmonize with the person of Christ is unsafe and is to be rejected no matter how plausible or rewarding it may seem to be. In any and all circumstances, we must stay true to and follow Christ's teachings and life pattern. Otherwise, we will be lost in the sea of conflicting ideas and religious practices.

Questions and Thoughts for Reflection

1. Perhaps you have been told that Phil. 4.13 has sometimes been called the superman verse and is translated "I can do all things through Him who strengthens me." However, this is very unlikely to be the correct translation of the Greek. The context must count strongly against such a rendering. Paul has been talking about perseverance and knowing how to carry on in good times and bad, knowing how to survive and endure in plenty and in want. Phil. 4.13 is further reflecting on godliness with contentment, a regular theme of Paul that he conveys to his converts. Obviously, we *cannot* do all things with the help of God's strength. We cannot leap tall buildings in a single bound, we cannot stand in front of a firing cannon and expect not to get hurt, and so on. The optimism expressed here is about perseverance and endurance. With God's help and strength, we can get through anything. We cannot just endure, we can prevail over difficult and dangerous circumstances, as Paul's own life provides example after example of.

The other major theme from this first lesson for this Sunday is that one can have confidence that God's purposes for and done through us will get accomplished. We can trust He will work all things together for good for those who love Him. Paul rightly trusted that all his many efforts for the Gospel would not be in vain. Do we have that sense of assurance that God is working our lives out in a good and godly way? Do we believe that we are part of a grand enterprise to redeem human beings and we have the privilege of having a part to play in a salvation plan that will not return to God null and void? Have we learned the lesson of how to get through good and bad times without losing our patience, our sanctification level, our trust in God? These are the questions we should reflect on based on this lesson.

2. Sometimes I have to laugh when people say that our country is more pagan than anything we have ever seen in the history of Christianity. This is simply not true. Paul lived in a robustly pagan environment where there was a belief in many, many gods, Greek and Roman gods, ancient Egyptian gods, and I could go on. Not only so but there were all sorts of behaviors including various sorts of sexual behaviors that were considered acceptable—like for instance pederasty by the master of the house with young slave boys in the household, or visiting prostitutes. In fact, the Greek word *porne* from which we get the word pornography has as its most basic meaning a prostitute. There is some positive news however to report.

Despite this overwhelmingly unbiblical environment, the Gospel was able to advance, to change many pagans into Christians despite the dominant ethos and values of the Greco-Roman world. Now you may say this was something of a miracle, and I would say yes, but then it will take miracles to change hearts and minds today. It takes a work of God's Spirit and grace today as well as in antiquity to redeem human beings. Our situation is not that different from in the time of St. Paul, and just as he didn't run around saying 'the sky is falling, and things can only get worse' neither should we do so. We need to get to work, Gospel work.

The second lesson of importance is Pop's discussion of decision-making based on what we know "squares with the character and the MO of Jesus." When things are not clear, and we can't cite a particular verse or verses for guidance, it is right to ask what Jesus would do under these circumstances. We used to hear WWJD a lot some decades ago and Christians even wore wristbands with this on it to remind us that we need to look to Christ's example for guidance. Unfortunately, we seem to have mostly forgotten about this, indeed the practice has even been ridiculed as trite or too simplistic. We see parodies like "What would Thor do" or "What would Spider-Man do." Jesus however was far different than either of these fictious superhero characters. Jesus didn't need to be a superhero; He was the savior. What is our attitude about our culture and its moral decline these days? How exactly should Christians respond to both an increasingly religiously pluralistic culture and an increasingly pagan culture? Can we take lessons and courage from the example of Paul and the success of early Christianity despite the pagan nature of that world of the first century AD? Think about these things.

Forty-sixth Sunday of the Year

5/18/69

"A new heart also I give you, and a new spirit will I put within you, and I will take away the heart of stone out of your flesh, and give you a heart of flesh." —Ezekiel 36.26

God is saying, through Ezekiel, I can give you a new heart. The heart all through the Scriptures stands for the control center of your being, the very seat of your soul. Your ego, your intelligence, your emotions are said to be in your heart or soul. God never does anything half way. Conversion means you get a new nature, a new control center of your personality and life. Jesus calls it "being born again," which involves repenting of sin and entering a new way of life. Have you had this encounter with Christ? Are you a new creature?

The Bible says all of us have sinned. You might not have committed all the sins in the book, but you have committed some—you are a sinner. We have all come short of the glory of God. We have failed to meet God's moral requirements. Every one of us has said or done wrong things sometime, somewhere. Everyone has had lust in his heart, sometime, somewhere. We have sinned against God (for every sin is a sin against God, though it may also be against our fellow human beings or even against ourselves) and this sin can cause physical, spiritual and even eternal death. I'm afraid many people, including many Christians, view sin in a trivial way. If its' not something major, it's not really a big deal or a sin with a capital S. How wrong they are, for there are as many sins of omission as there are sins of commission, both less and more severe. "We have all sinned and fallen short of the glory of God," says Paul.

When we stay away from God's house for petty or selfish reasons, we are letting our sinful inclinations take over in our lives. God cannot accept you when that sinful inclination has taken over. You would not fit in heaven. It would not even be heaven to you, for you would be miserable there, it would be hell to you because you would be different from the others there. The excuse for not attending church is one thing. But the real reason is because your sinful inclinations have taken over your behavior, and it is keeping you away not only from worshipping God, but from God Himself!

There is a great hue and cry for justice in our land these days, and it is understandable. But if we are talking about divine justice, justice from God, trust me, you who are a sinner do not want that. Justice is when you get what you deserve, and what the sinner deserves is judgment. We should rather all be asking for God's mercy. In the cross of Christ, we see both the mercy of God, which is when we do not get what we actually deserve as sinners, but there is more in the cross—there is the love of God and the grace of God. Grace is when we instead get something positive from God which we do not deserve and have no earned. Instead of justice, we get mercy and love and grace from God. What a God we have!

But it's not just a matter of God declaring us free from condemnation. It is about God changing our nature, of giving us the new birth, so at last our stony hearts are replaced with a heart of flesh, capable of loving God with all we are and all we have, and loving our fellow human beings as well. It is not enough to be declared not guilty. We must also be changed into the likeness of Christ, and it begins with a new heart.

11/1/70

"For all things come from Thee, and of thy own we have given back to thee." —1 Chronicles 29.14

Is there in all our language a better word than "stewardship" to sum up the Christian spirit in worship and work? For all that we have and all that we are or hope to be comes from God. We are not owners of anything, we are only stewards of God's property, including our very selves. As Christians, we owe to Christ all our possessions of whatever kind. We hold them in trust for Him. They are ours *pro tempore* for the time being during this brief life to be administered for Him and according to His will, but we are never in absolute ownership of anything. And some day we must give an accounting to God for what we have done with things, including with our very lives. "Our souls are our own" is a great untruth for soul and body must be presented at the last day before Christ's throne. We have been bought with a price, and we are not our own.

Therefore, let us not be unrighteous stewards, withholding from God that which is His due, trifling with His gifts, or misusing the talents He has entrusted to us. Rather let us strive to render to Him the full measure of our service, saying within our hearts "all things have come from Thee." If it is a great responsibility, it is no less a glorious privilege allotted to us in His divine plan. We are trustees of God's gifts, agents of Christ.

In fact, that is why we are here on earth. God puts His confidence in us, expecting our loyal obedience. He died that we might live with Him forever. If we have our hands in the firm grip of the Father's hands everlasting life is ours. So let us rededicate ourselves this day and every day, praising Him in our lives as well as with our lips, growing by and in His grace, in holiness and righteousness, to be made like unto Him.

Are we good stewards? He does keep a record book you know. He knows even our thoughts, as well as our words and deeds and will reward us according to our merits. His eye is on the sparrow, and I know He watches me.

Questions and Thoughts for Reflection

1. The ancients believed that the heart was the control center of human beings. It was the center of thought, feeling, will. There is a reason the Psalmist says "cleanse the thoughts of my heart by the inspiration of your Spirit." Of course, today we know that the heart is a pump and the brain is the control center of human personality. So,

when we hear about God giving us a new heart, what we are talking about is a fundamental change in our thoughts, feelings, will in regard to God and His plans for humanity and for us as individuals.

Sin by definition is a violation of God's will, and all of us are sinners to one degree or another. Any sin if not repented of, can separate us from God in some ways, or at least alienate us from God. It is odd, but nonetheless true that some Christians think if they have not broken the major commandments then they are not really sinners with a capital S. The problem with this is that the sins of the heart—the lust, the greed, the pride, the hatred—are just as serious as the sins of action, and then there are all the sins of omission as well. Trust me, there is no such thing as a person who has not committed sins for which Jesus had to die.

I was once shown the illustration of a glass of water and an eyedropper with red dye in it. Even just one drop of the die colored all the water. Sin is like that. It taints everything. Our posture in relationship to God should be like the man in the parable—"Lord, have mercy on me, a sinner." So how do you both view and deal with the sin in your life? Do you make a regular practice of confession? Have you had a born-again experience in which God changed your life orientation and way of thinking and feeling about life? What is the most important change that happened in your life as result of loving Christ?

2. We have already had occasion to talk about stewardship, but it is difficult to get Americans to give up the notion that they are owners of things when in fact "the earth is the Lord's and the fullness thereof." One way to think about this is that you are only "owners" in a loose sense of whatever you brought with you into this world at birth and whatever you take with you at death. In other words, no material possessions that you have accumulated between birth and death really belong to you, properly speaking. You are merely stewards of God's property. See my book *Jesus and Money*. It is interesting that there are lots of mistaken notions about stewardship in the church. If you read closely Acts 2–6 what stewardship meant back then and there was "no exclusive right to property." It meant that on principle

you were prepared to share in common what you had, but you were still individually in charge of the decision what and how much to share. The early church made sure no one went without the basics—food, shelter, clothing, and so should we. But as the story of Ananias and Sapphira also makes clear it was up to them to decide how much to give and when it came to their possessions. Peter says, "Was it not still in your possession after you had sold the property and had been paid?" The answer to that question was yes.

And similarly, in Acts 2 and 4 each gave as they were able and decided to do, not claiming any exclusive right to what they possessed, but rather sharing to make sure no one was in want or need. And as for those especially prone to being indigent, they set up a special team and resources to take care of the widows. None of this should be labeled communism, but it is also at odds with modern secular theories of capitalism and private ownership (to be distinguished from private possessions about which one applies stewardship principles). Sometimes the notion of charity becomes pretty unchristian, because the assumption behind it is "what's mine is mine, and if I choose to share some it, I'm being charitable." Actually, it's not optional to share with others and be generous because actually whatever you have is a gift from God of which you are to be a good steward. Does this make sense to you? Reread Acts 2–6 and think about what it implies about a theory of property and stewardship. Have you in the past been a good steward of your resources, or have you rather regularly squandered them on trivial things or selfish pursuits?

Forty-seventh Sunday of the Year

5/25/69

"At the same time the disciples came to Jesus saying 'who is the greatest in the kingdom of heaven?' And Jesus called a little child unto him, and set him in the midst of them. And said 'Truly I say to you, except you turn/be converted and become as a little child, you shall not enter into the kingdom of heaven.'" —Matthew 18.1-3

What about this word turn or convert? The disciples came to Jesus and said, "Who is going to be first in your kingdom, Jesus?" But Jesus had already told them, "He who would be first, must be last and the servant of all." The requirement for entrance into heaven is true humility, not false piety, but a true and genuine humility.[5] This requirement recognizes both our need and our sin, and also recognizes the greatness of the majesty of God, and a willingness to accept Christ as Savior. So, to illustrate the point, Jesus called a little child to Him and said, "Look at this little child, how trusting this child is, how humble this child is. Before you can get to heaven, you must become converted and behave like a little child. You must go back to your childhood. You must trust in God with the same simplicity and same humility and same dependence that a little child has for his parents." In other words, the conversion He is talking about is a change in direction, a turning to a totally different direction—to turn around, to change.

---

5. Jesus is not talking about entrance into heaven. He is talking about when God's kingdom comes on earth as it is in heaven in the future.

A famous psychologist once said that this generation needs converting more than any generation in history. Another psychologist recently said we are so psychologically constituted as to need converting, and if the church fails to change people, we psychologists are going to have to do it. So even psychology is recognizing the need for human beings to be converted. The Bible teaches that you must be converted to enter God's Kingdom. The psychologist teaches you must be converted to get the most out of life. The big question for each of us to ask ourselves is "Have we become as little children?" Have we really been converted to Jesus Christ? Do we know that we have done so and are sure? The Bible stresses, "If anyone is in Christ, he is a new creature." Have you had this renewal experience in your life?

2/7/71

"Come unto me, all you that labor and are heavy laden and I will give you rest." —Matthew 11.28

This is a wonderful promise that should be sounded throughout the entire world. The world needs it worse now than ever before. It is a positive announcement that is absolute in nature. Jesus stands ready to give every human being the gift of peace, and the gift of rest. He gives us four great thoughts to guide us in life without error.

Every direction Jesus gives for this life could be traced as the product of either honesty or kindness. Those are two great thoughts for this life. The practices they suggest would fill the world with light and peace. For the life to come, He tells us our sins are pardoned. His death upon Calvary paid the debt of each one of the children of humanity, yes for all people. Any day, anyone can begin the new life in Christ.

The cross of Jesus tells the great truth, the old debt of sin is paid. Our sins are forgiven. The other thought that has to do with the life beyond, is God's glorious promise of heaven. No one but Jesus gives us this plan. You and I are very foolish if we do not accept this plan of life in its fullness. It is our duty to make it our business to lead others to accept Jesus and His great thoughts. We should never give up on

God in Christ. If we have given Him up, we need to turn, we need to come back to Him now while there is life and time to do so. He will answer our life's questions as no one else can. He will give us rest, so lead as many as you can to Him. He will give everyone inspiration, and peace, and rest. He never fails.

Questions and Thoughts for Reflection

1. It has been said that we are called to childlike faith, but not a childish one. What is the difference? The sort of thing Jesus is talking about is having a simple trust in and dependency on God, just as a small child has on his parents. But especially in a senior and male-dominated culture like the one Jesus lived in, turning and becoming like a child in approach and attitude may well have seemed demeaning to Jesus' inner circle of male disciples. Notice that in a parallel story the male disciples try to prevent people from bothering Jesus with their small children. And in this same context they had asked who is the greatest in the Kingdom? Clearly, they are not on the same wavelength as Jesus in regard to:1) what constitutes greatness, and 2) what it takes to enter the Kingdom of God.

My grandfather is right that part of the key is humility. It is interesting that the Greek word in question for "humility" was normally pejorative. It means to act like a slave, to be subservient to others. This was not seen as a virtue in the Greco-Roman world, but it certainly is in the Bible. The key to greatness is to become the servant of all. The key to entrance into the kingdom is turning and becoming like a child—dependent on and trusting in God. Both of these things offend the pride of arrogant human beings, and this included, apparently, some of the disciples as well with their macho idea of what makes a person great and fit to be in the kingdom with Jesus, indeed fit to sit on His right and His left. What in your view is the difference between genuine humility and humiliation? How does our culture define greatness and how does that contrast with Jesus' definition?

2. If we were to look at the whole saying in question in Matt. 11, we would discover the paradoxical claim by Jesus that He is offering an easy yoke and a light burden! He does not say it won't be a yoke, and

He doesn't say it won't be a burden. He does say that if you do what He says namely come unto me and assume the yoke and burden He offers, He will give you rest. How does one get rest from assuming a yoke and a burden? The disciples will have known very well that yokes are onerous things, heavy, burdensome. A yoke is the kind of thing you put on your ox to plow the field or go round and round the millstone grinding the grain. But of course, Jesus is not talking about a literal yoke. He is using the term metaphorically just as Paul later calls someone his true yokefellow.

Perhaps Jesus is doing a comparison. He knows the audience is laboring and heavy laden, and He offers something a bit lighter. But if that is what He meant it seems to be at odds with His other call—namely take up your cross daily and follow me. A cross is not a light burden. So what is Jesus really getting at? You need to know the context.

If you were to go back and read the popular Jewish wisdom book called Sirach, you would discover that the term yoke was used of the Mosaic Law. *Sirach* 51:26 says, "Put your neck under her *yoke*, and let your souls receive instruction; it is to be found close by." So, in fact Jesus is suggesting that His teaching is less burdensome and produces more rest than the Mosaic Law. This is not because it was less demanding. It is because it is the teaching which when embraced and lived gives genuine *shalom*—wholeness, wellness, peace. The Hebrew word for all these three things is *shalom*. There is perhaps also a second hidden promise here that if you embrace Jesus and "his yoke" your quest for the meaning of life, for everlasting life, for peace and rest from all the struggle to live life will reach its proper goal. So how restful or peaceful is your life? Do you have the satisfaction of knowing you are following the right sort of religious instruction, and the right teacher—Jesus Himself? Notice Jesus didn't promise that there wouldn't be burdens. What He promised is that if following Him is truly embraced, He will give us rest, peace, shalom, everlasting life. What could be better than that?

Forty-eighth Sunday of the Year

"And now abides faith, hope, and love, these three, but the greatest of these is love." —1 Corinthians 13.13

Love is the greatest among the Christian graces. Eloquence is powerful, but unless there is a personality of love and emotion in back of it, it is as meaningless as the noise of sounding brass and clanging cymbals. Benevolent and charitable deeds are praiseworthy only when they are prompted by the spirit of love. Giving to the poor may be prompted by selfish desire to gain honor or power. True martyrdom registers the temperature of Christian devotion, but many a bad cause has its martyrs. Some may worship an individual, or money, or golf, or football, or gambling, or drink, or they are just drifting aimlessly away from God with no real reason. They are just careless and unconcerned. Or do they stay away from God's house because of some gossip that they accept without trying to find out the real truth of the matter? Love overcomes all these things.

Love quenches that spirit of envy and jealousy which seeks to belittle the success and achievements of others. The spirit of self-exaltation and self-interest finds no place in love's lexicon. Unselfishness and self-forgetfulness always mark the activities of the love impelled Christian. Love is, quite deliberately, a poor bookkeeper or grudge holder. In the formulation of its program, true Christian love is so profoundly concerned with the triumph of righteousness, it is absolutely uninterested in the petty excuses we use, trying to justify our ego. Christian love grows. It never dies. It is permanent and abiding. Many things continue for a time and then vanish away or slip from our grasp. Earthly possessions are unstable. Even human friendships are subject to disruption. Life itself is uncertain as far as its duration on earth is concerned.

Christian love is not temporary. As for permanence it is even greater than faith and hope. Faith may be lost within the eyesight, or better said faith will one day turn to sight. Hope ends in fruition, but surely love will only grow stronger as the anticipated glories of the future world become the permanent possession of the Christian believer. Where do we stand? How strong is our love for God and our fellow human beings?

10/17/71

"Blessed are the pure in heart, for they shall see God." —Matthew 5.8

The world says seeing is believing. The Word says, believing is seeing. Sight and insight these are the marks of a man of the world and a man of God. Think of it—to be cultured and capable, yet not to know the Savior nor to understand God's Word. The eye is not the only organ of sight. To see the unseen is the difference between the mind of the spirit and the mind of the flesh. Think of Elisha hemmed in by a host of enemies. To his servant that was the only thing he could see. But the prophet saw behind the veil, saw that the mountain was full of horses and chariots of fire. The forces which were seen were only a fragment of the warring hosts. Spiritual forces were on the march.

When we are hard pressed, we need to look up. There is a famous Norman Rockwell painting of the front of a church titled *Lift Up Thine Eyes* that powerfully punctuates this point. The church sign announces the sermon title "Lift Up Thine Eyes," but the crowds on the street below are downcast and not paying attention to God's call to them. It is a powerful parable of our time.

Jesus still anoints human eyes. Seeing is not looking on the outside of things. Seeing is discerning the meaning of life and things. Christ came unto the world that in Him people might get a glimpse of God and His very nature or character. Such a vision steadies us in trials, comforts us in sorrow, and makes our life rich and full.

Faith is knowledge, a spiritual and superior sort of knowledge. The Gospel is not against reason, only above reason. A writer once said, the heart has reasons that reason knows not of. The purification of the heart brings with it the best that is in humankind, and as the beatitude says because their faith is unquestionable and unwavering they shall see God.

Questions and Thoughts for Reflection

1. There are two subjects on which my grandfather was most eloquent—on the Bible being God's Word, and on Christian love. Our first lesson for this Sunday is about the latter of these subjects—focus on what Pop says here: "Love quenches that spirit of envy and jealousy which seeks to belittle the success and achievements of others. The spirit of self-exaltation and self-interest finds no place in love's lexicon. Unselfishness and self-forgetfulness always mark the activities of the love impelled Christian. Love is, quite deliberately, a poor bookkeeper or grudge holder. In the formulation of its program, true Christian love is so profoundly concerned with the triumph of righteousness, it is absolutely uninterested in the petty excuses we use, trying to justify our ego. Christian love grows. It never dies. It is permanent and abiding."

Love keeps no record of wrongdoing. How very hard that is to do if you have been badly wronged. But again, Paul is not assuming we do this in our own strength, he is assuming God's love poured into our hearts makes the difficult possible. And another thing, it is one thing to be just plain forgetful, but it is a Christian thing to be self-forgetful. In an egotistic and self-centered culture, you really have to work at self-forgetfulness because all the advertising in the world is encouraging us to be self-indulgent.

If you were to take a personal inventory of your own behavior, and at the same time ask one person who knows you best to do the same, and in each case ask, how loving and self-sacrificial is this person, how well do you think the answers from the two inventories would match up? Socrates was right that we do indeed need to know ourselves. But from a Christian point of view, the key to that is knowing God, and knowing how He evaluates us. One way to do that is to read slowly through Psalm 139.1-18 and ask yourself how much do you identify with the Psalmist and what he says.

2. The story of Elijah seeing the angelic chariots which his servant could not see is a powerful story about the difference between seeing things with merely human eyes, and seeing things with spiritual eyes. Too often we only look at the visible things, and overlook the invisible and spiritual things like love and God. Too seldom do we pray for spiritual sight and insight when we are faced with a difficult situation. Sometimes when I go jogging I keep my eyes looking down in case I might trip on something and fall. But there are also times when I need to look up, because here comes traffic or a bicycle. The Bible, interestingly enough, doesn't tell us to look down in a self-protective way, rather it often exhorts us to "lift up our eyes" to the Lord. I love the Norman Rockwell painting which illustrates how seldom people look up to God despite the Biblical exhortations. What about you? Do you have the faith to look up and the spiritual eyes to see what God is doing in a situation? Some Christians are better than others in discerning God's activity and involvement in a situation. It is a spiritual gift. Blessed are those who see with God's eyes.

Forty-ninth Sunday of the Year

4/6/69

"And when they were come unto a place called Golgotha, the place called the Skull, they gave Jesus vinegar to drink mingled with myrrh, and when he had tasted it, he would not drink it, and they crucified Him." —Matthew 27.33

Look at Jesus on the cross. Here were evil, vengeful men spitting on Him, mocking Him, taunting Him, all unjustly. As He looked at them, He saw the hatred in their faces, violence in their hands, foul language on their lips, and blackness in their hearts. Nothing could have called for a greater negative reaction than all that. But what did Jesus do? He said, "Father forgive them, for they know not what they do." You may say, well yes, but He was Jesus and I am just a normal person. If you are a Christian with Christ living in your heart, you are not just a normal person! You have the greatest superhuman power known on earth—the power to forgive.

Paul wrote to the Colossians who were harassed on every hand, unjustly. He says Christ is all, and He is in all. He reminds them that their bodies are temples of Christ, the actual abode of the Savior. Then he said, "Put on therefore as the elect of God, holy and beloved, deep feelings of compassion, of mercy, or forgiveness as Christ did. To that add kindness, humility, meekness, long suffering, forbearing one another. If anyone has a quarrel against another, forgive the other seven times or seventy times seven if they ask for it, even as Christ has perpetually forgiven you, so you also must forgive. If Christ lives in us, we will do precisely as He did on the cross and under severe duress. We are to judge not lest we be judged. If our love for Christ is genuine, we will always work for the best interest of His Kingdom and His church. He says love thy neighbor as thyself, and He also said 'take up your cross and follow me" (Mark 8.34 and par). Are we bearing our crosses for Him?

"Forgetting the things that are behind, and reaching forth unto those things which are before us . . ." —Philippians 3.13

Here Paul speaks relatively, for he would not have us forget everything. He was never able to do that himself. After he had stood never protesting at the stoning of Stephen and had ravaged the infant church in Jerusalem and Judaea its early days, I do not doubt that ghosts of his early days as a young man made him always humble. But he deliberately placed the emphasis upon the present and the future.

Yesterday, for better or worse, was over and gone. Today, now, this very minute is upon us. We are sure of it. The past will never return. What then of today and tomorrow? That is the thing to emphasize. Place tomorrow with its hopes, its opportunities, its possibilities in the foreground. We do well to forget old sins, for true repentance brings forgiveness. Then, even as God does, we can remember them no more.

We also do well to forget old failures, except as we have the gumption to extract their lessons and apply them to the future. We do well to forget old griefs. The only incurable sorrow is a coddled sorrow, a sorrow that has been nursed to the point that one is having a pity party. Our best tribute to love ones vanished from our sight is not our tears but our emulation of their virtues. The finest thing we can do for them is to make their best ideals come true.

What the years shall bring, only God knows. Next year may be much like other years for us, or it may bring a beautiful future, or it may bring calamity. There will be in it, doubtless, both joy and grief. There will likely be clouds, but clouds before they vanish may form great white castles in the sky, and rainbows are impossible without clouds. Now is the accepted time. With grateful hearts, we own our pasts. We do not know what the future hold but we know who holds the future in His guardian care, and we leave it in His hands.

We have a new day, week, or year—what will it bring? We read in the Bible Christ makes all things new. Because of this hope, this mortal and mundane existence becomes less to be concerned about, less to worry about in the light of eternity. God has reconciled the world to Himself in Christ and has made us ambassadors and agents of that reconciliation. Life is too short, hell is too hot, and heaven is too wonderful for us to trifle with our souls, or make our lives a game of trivial pursuit.

Questions and Thoughts for Reflection

1. The story of Christ's request that His tormentors be forgiven whilst He was hanging on the cross, is perhaps the most poignant of all the seven last sayings of Christ from the cross. And my grandfather is right—the instinctive human reaction to that scene is, "Well, that was Jesus, I am not cut from the same cloth as He was." But this forgets that Jesus told Peter he also must practice unlimited forgiveness when he has been wronged. It was not just something for a divine person like Jesus to do. It is something for us to do as well, but only by the empowering grace and love of God can we do it. One of the things to be learned from that scene on the cross is that we are to follow Christ's example and be proactive rather than reactive to a situation especially a difficult one.

I think my grandfather is right that forgiveness is one of the most powerful forces on earth. It is all the more powerful when there is something major to forgive. After the end of apartheid in South Africa, there was the remarkable Truth and Reconciliation Commission. At its hearings, Afrikaners who had tortured and killed black Africans were given the chance to come and confess their crimes, and be forgiven, and then suffer no further consequences. It is amazing to watch those hearing and see what truth and forgiveness can do. You can get a little insight into this by watching Tom Wright's DVD titled *EVIL*. It turns out, Christians have a power from God to change others' lives who have hurt them by forgiveness. Have you ever had occasion to practice forgiveness? Of course, forgiveness is one thing, and reconciliation is another, but forgiveness opens the door to a fresh start, especially if coupled with repentance and forgiveness.

2. I agree with the adage that you can't live in the past for its gone, but you can learn from it. It is true that the earliest Christians stood on tiptoe looking forward to what was coming, including the anticipated return of Christ. Some Christians today let their past spoil their present and future. John Ed Mathison tells the story of a faithful Christian lady in his church who was always a ray of sunshine, until her husband ran off with a woman half his wife's age, and a root of bitterness grew up in her heart. Instead of getting better after the divorce, she got increasingly bitter. Finally, John Ed could stand it no more as it was ruining her life and poisoning her relationships in the church so he called her into the office one day and said, "Now Betty, we are going to try an experiment to see if you can get beyond what happened a year ago with your husband. I want you to imagine he is sitting in a chair right across from you and I want you to tell John that you forgive him." She looked shocked, but knew she should do it, so she said in the angriest tone she could muster I FORGIVE YOU! And then she spat in the direction of that chair. "Well," said John Ed, "it's a start. Let's try that again with a little less venom." She repeated what she said before at a lower volume, and without spitting. "Better," said John Ed. "Now I want you to imagine Jesus sitting right next to John, the Jesus who said from the cross to His tormentors, "I forgive you, for you know not what you are doing." At this Betty began to whimper, and then the tears really began to flow. In what was barely a whisper Betty said, "John, I forgive you with the help of Jesus." Then John Ed said, "Now let him and it go Betty because nursing that wound is poisoning your life." That was the turning point for Betty. She went forward getting better rather than more bitter. And the lesson in this example is that forgiveness offered by the wounded Christian is as important for healing as forgiveness received, indeed it is important even if the offender never receives it, or never even realizes he needs it! Forgiveness offered is one thing, forgiveness received is another. What examples can you think of where forgiveness has made a big difference in someone's life?

Fiftieth Sunday of the Year

Christmastide
12/22/68

"For unto us a child is born, unto us a Son is given, and the government shall be upon his shoulders, and his name shall be called wonderful counselor, mighty God, everlasting Father, the prince of peace." —Isaiah 9:6

In all the Scriptures there is no more thrilling a passage than that found in the ninth chapter of Isaiah. Here the Savior, Jesus was named wonderful. He was wonderful already in His pre-existence. When the Pharisees boasted of their ancestor Abraham, Jesus replied 'Before Abraham was, I am.' He was called the lamb of God slain from the foundation of the world. He is the only person in heaven or on earth equally at home in either realm. He mingled with sinners but was sinless, He consorted with the rich and yet was untainted by their gold, and the record tells us He once said, "The Son of Man has nowhere to lay his head." He associated with tax collectors and sinners but never partook of their sins. Even His worst enemies could not find a single flaw in His reproachless character.

He was called counselor, and if ever the world needed the counsel of Christ it is today. Thousands of individuals all over the world who have accepted Him as their divine Advocate have found a solution to their baffling problems. I know that many of the world's leaders could tell you that in Christ they have found a divine counselor to help guide the affairs of human beings.

Isaiah prophesied that the messiah's name would be Prince of Peace. The craving and desire for peace is universal. It is part and parcel of our very nature to want to live in tranquility, free from confusions, discord, and strife.

12/5/76

"This is how the birth of Jesus the Messiah came about—His mother Mary was pledged to be married to Joseph, but before they came together, she was found to be pregnant through the Holy Spirit. Because Joseph her husband was faithful to the law, and yet did not want to expose her to public disgrace, he had in mind to divorce her quietly." —Matthew 1.18-19

This month the entire Christian world is looking to a lowly manger filled with straw in Bethlehem, to an event that happened about two thousand years ago. It was an event that changed the course of human history. A baby was born that was so important that the angels attended, and even wise men from the East traveled far to come and worship Him. This child was born in Judaea and grew up in Nazareth in Galilee.

The Scriptures give only a little glimpse of Mary and Joseph before Christ was born. Joseph was a religious man and evidence shows that Mary had a thorough knowledge of the Scriptures. This is perhaps one reason that God selected her to be the mother of Jesus, even though she was only a teenager. God was pleased with her.

Mary was betrothed to Joseph, but before they came together as a man and wife, she was found to be with child by means of the Holy Spirit. But Mary and Joseph had kept their engagement of love pure. Joseph then planned to break their engagement quietly, as he was a good man. But then the angel came to him and explained the situation. The angel said, "Do not fear to take Mary as your wife, for that which was conceived was of the Holy Spirit." The angel told Joseph that Mary would give birth to a son and His name would be Jesus, and He would be the Savior of His people. Joseph was well satisfied as he believed God.

So Christ was born, truly man and yet He was more than a man, He was the Son of God who had come to live among humankind, and thus we have the first Christmas. The name Jesus Christ blossoms on the pages of history like flowers of a thousand spring times. That name will echo down the corridors of time forever.

Questions and Thoughts for Reflection

1. The prophecies in Isaiah 7, 9, and 11 have long been part of the Christmas story. They are also part of the libretto of lyrics that George Fredrich Handel received, which inspired him to write his greatest work, simply called *Messiah*. Like many musicians of his age, he lived hand to mouth. He had tried writing operas for the opera houses in Italy with little success. He moved to England to try and get a position as a court musician and he wrote *The Royal Fireworks* for a royal event which helped get him noticed. He, like King George, was from Hanover in Germany, and this apparently helped him get commissions from the court, for example like his famous piece called *Water Music*. But by the time he set out to write his *Messiah*, he was once again financially in a pinch.

The libretto so inspired him that he spent day and night and day and night in his rented rooms in London composing the music, and when he got to the Hallelujah chorus near the end of the work, he ran out of his room and said to his landlady, "I did think I saw all heaven before me and the Great God himself." *Messiah* was to go on to be his greatest work, even though initially the reviews were mixed. John Wesley went to an early performance of *Messiah* and commented in his journal on August 17, 1758, "I went to the [Bristol] cathedral to hear Mr. Handel's *Messiah*. I doubt if that congregation was ever so serious at a sermon as they were during this performance." Apparently, it had a dramatic effect on some audiences, even more so than a good sermon.

The various prophecies in Isaiah have led to the book being called The Fifth Gospel, and with good reason too. Isaiah is by far the most cited, alluded to, or echoed Old Testament book in the New Testament, well ahead of the Psalms which have the second most citations, and then, thirdly, portions of the Pentateuch. It is clear enough in our lessons for today that Matthew thought that these Isaianic prophecies were fulfilled in the life of Christ, even in the most surprising parts of His life—the miraculous conception, and the atoning death. One exercise I would encourage everyone to do is to read through Isaiah 7, 9, and 11 during the Christmas season and go see the performance of the Christmas portion of Handel's *Messiah*. It will enhance your Christmas celebration as much as any Christmas pageant. Music can convey types of meaning in a way that mere words cannot. It can stir the emotions as well as the mind. Are you prepared to celebrate Christmas in a Christian way?

2. The commercialization of Christmas (the busiest shopping season of the year) has led without question to an overly materialistic approach to Christmas, which has often dampened or dulled the proper spiritual emphasis and meaning of the season. Disturbed by this overlay of materialism at Christmas I wrote the following poem. See what you think.

The Bonding

A cold and listless season,
And full of cheerless cheer,
When hopes are raised and dashed again
And joy dissolves in tears.

The search for endless family
The search for one true Friend
Leaves questers tired, disconsolate
With questions without end.

Best find some potent pleasure quick
Some superficial thrill
Then search for everlasting love
When none can fill that bill.

So hide yourselves in shopping
And eating 'til you burst,
Use endless entertainment
As shelter from the worst.

And hope at least for truce on earth,
Though warlords rattle swords

FIFTIETH SUNDAY OF THE YEAR

As if to kill could solve our ills
We seize our "just" rewards.

Mistake some rest for lasting peace
And calm for "all is well"
And absence of activity
As year end's victory bell.

But what if Advent is no quest
Despite the wise men's star
What if Advent isn't reached
By driving from afar?

What if Good News comes to us
From well beyond our reach?
What if love and peace on earth
Are more than things we preach?

What if a restless peace
Is what He did intend
Until we open up our lives
And let the stranger in?

What if a peaceless rest
Is not the Christmas hope
What if nothing we could do
Helps us truly cope?

What if there is a bonding
With one who rules above
Who came to us in beggar's rags
And brought the gift of love?

The God shaped hole in every heart
Is healed by just one source
When Jesus comes to claim his own
Who are without recourse.

So give up endless seeking
Surrender is required
The one who is the Lord of all
Cannot be bought or hired.

He's not conjured into life
By pomp and circumstance
By Yuletide carols boldly sung
By fun or drunken trance.

He comes unbidden, unawares
Fills crevices of souls
He comes on his own timely terms
And makes the sinner whole.

"We shall be restless" said the saint
"Until we rest in thee"
And find that we have been reborn,
Our own nativity.

How silently, how silently
The precious truth is given
And God imparts to human hearts
The blessings of his heaven.

While I have no desire to be the Grinch that stole Christmas, I do think that the church especially needs to de-enculturate itself from some of the things alluded to in this poem, for they are soul deadening rather than soul nourishing. What is your reaction to this suggestion and to the poem?

Fifty-first Sunday of the Year

12/11/77

"The angel went to her and said, 'Greetings, you who are highly favored! The Lord is with you.' Mary was greatly troubled at his words and wondered what kind of greeting this might be. But the angel said to her, 'Do not be afraid, Mary; you have found favor with God. You will conceive and give birth to a son, and you are to call him Jesus. He will be great and will be called the Son of the Most High. The Lord God will give him the throne of his father David, and he will reign over Jacob's descendants forever; his kingdom will never end.' 'How will this be,' Mary asked the angel, 'since I am a virgin?' The angel answered, 'The Holy Spirit will come on you, and the power of the Most High will overshadow you. So the holy one to be born will be called the Son of God. Even Elizabeth your relative is going to have a child in her old age, and she who was said to be unable to conceive is in her sixth month. For no word from God will ever fail.' 'I am the Lord's servant,' Mary answered. 'May your word to me be fulfilled.' Then the angel left her." —Luke 1.28-38

The virgin birth is a mere trifle for God. That God should become man is a greater miracle, but most amazing of all is that this maiden named Mary should get credit. That she, rather than some other virgin, had been chosen by God to be the mother of the messiah is surprising. But Mary gloried solely in God's gracious regard.

Mary then went and stayed with Elizabeth for about three months, for Elizabeth was already with child. She and her husband Zechariah were old, but God promised them a child, and made this possible for them. Elizabeth's child was to be John the Baptizer, the forerunner of Jesus, preparing the way for His coming.

Joseph when he heard of Mary's pregnancy was very disturbed. Her condition caused him to be puzzled as to what to do, and if he followed the law of the day he would have had to denounce her. But God spoke to Joseph through an angel in a dream and he was told to fear not for there was no dishonor or disgrace to take Mary as his wife for "she is with child by means of the Holy Spirit." Joseph took God's Word for it, and he accepted the unusual situation and married Mary, for he was a devout man.

Elizabeth baby was born in God's favor and with His blessings. You see this too was a part of God's plan, namely that John would grow up to be the forerunner of Jesus, going from place to place preaching, preparing the way for the coming of the Lord. Many people thought that John himself might be the messiah, so he had to keep telling people that it was not him, but the one who came after him, who amazingly was in another sense before John. John said he baptized with water, but the one who came after him would baptize them with the Holy Spirit, and that he was only a servant not even worthy to unlace the sandals from that greater one's feet.

John was indeed a prophet of God sent to open the way of salvation with the people so that they could freely and without fear serve God. God had promised these downtrodden people that He would free them so that they might have peace, for He is a merciful God and is willing and glad to forgive if they would only trust Him. The question is, do we trust Him in the same way and to the same degree as Mary and Joseph who risked scandal to obey God?

12/2/79

"The Word took on flesh . . ." —John 1.14

Desiring His children to know Him, to possess His life, to live in the light of His presence, God took on flesh. When the Master was upon the earth, we hear Him say "I am the way" not "I show the way." Then He says "I am the truth" not "I teach the truth," then He says

"I am the life" not "I reveal the life." No other great teacher has ever been able so to speak, because no other was God in the flesh.

About one third of the people in the world are professing Christians. Nearly all the remaining two thirds have some form of faith. When we read the news we are faced with different modes of religion in the Middle East. While Confucianism is more of a system of ethics than a religion, it is the only religion many millions know about. Buddhism is accepted by many more. Islam is the faith of great multitudes. These people revere the memory of their founder, Mohammed, but they know he was just a man and is dead. But Christianity is a faith in one who was and is alive. Jesus is the same yesterday, today and forever. He is nearer to believers today than He was when He walked the earth. One of His last messages was, "I will be with you today and forever."

Whenever the truth of the living presence of the Lord has been grasped, it has resulted in remarkable changes. The same power that has revolutionized individuals and community lives in the past is at work in the world today. By claiming the promise of His presence, we will see transformed lives and a changed world. Each person can help and must help if this is to be achieved. He gave His all for us, what will we give to Him?

Questions and Thoughts for Reflection

1 and 2. In the Catholic form of Christianity, one prayer that many Catholics pray regularly is actually the words of the angel, "Hail Mary, full of grace," but this is a translation from the Latin, which is not exactly a good representation of the Greek which basically says. "Greetings Mary, you who are highly favored by God." Scholars and lay people for centuries have pondered why this young Jewish girl was picked to be the mother of the messiah. The debate still goes on. What we can say is that Luke's account, which contrasts the reaction of Zechariah to the angel when he is in the temple in Jerusalem with the reaction of Mary to the angel in Galilee, provides us with a clue. Mary's response is one of absolute submission and faith—"be it unto me as you had said, I am the handmaiden of the Lord." This response however comes after the explanation of HOW this would

happen—namely by a miraculous impregnation by means of the Holy Spirit. Contrast this with the doubting HOW CAN THIS BE of Zechariah who thinks he and Elizabeth are far too old for such a thing happening. Zechariah is struck dumb because he doesn't take the angel at his word. Mary is blessed and gets an explanation and a commendation from the angel. Mary is in fact depicted as a model of how a disciple should respond to the divine message. Zechariah, not so much.

If we ask the question why exactly there needed to be a virginal conception, the typical theological answer has been because Jesus needed to come into the world without inherited original sin, an idea based on the assumption that the sperm of the man was the carrier of human fallenness. If we ask what about Mary, wasn't she also a fallen human being, one response would be that even if so, the Spirit sanctified her womb when she was impregnated. So, the virginal conception deals with the fallenness factor affecting human nature, and so the preexistent Son of God takes on pure flesh in the womb of Mary. Incarnation happens by means of virginal conception, as the Son continues to be divine but takes on a human nature.

The best translation of the lesson from today is "and the Word took on flesh" because the Word did not turn into flesh. There was not an exchange of the one for the other. What there was, was divine self-limitation of the Son of God so He could be fully human as well as fully divine. He did not take on human fallenness or sin at the incarnation, but He did take on the normal human limitations we experience—limitations of time, space, knowledge, power, and mortality. Jesus' life was not a charade in which He pretended to be human. When He says in Mark 13.32 He doesn't know the timing of the second coming He is not crossing His fingers behind His back. When we hear in Lk. 2.41-52 that He grew in knowledge or wisdom over time, this is because He did. When Jesus was in Nazareth He was not also in Capernaum. In other words, He put the omnis (omniscience, omnipotence, omnipresence) on hold when He took on flesh.

Notice that the temptations Jesus faced in the wilderness were not normal human temptations. Satan was tempting Him to push the God button. We do not have a God button. Jesus did and He refused to push it, because it would have ruined His true humanity. No normal person would be tempted to turn stones into bread, though I've known a few cooks who could turn bread into stones. Notice Jesus resisted temptation by citing Scripture and relying on the help of the Spirit, just as believers do. Notice as well that He performs His miracles by the power of the Spirit, including His exorcisms, the same power that enabled His disciples to later do miracles. Here at Christmas time, it is not only appropriate, it is crucial that we better understand both the humanity and the divinity of Christ. He was 100% both, not 90% human and 10% divine or vice versa The very reason Paul and others can tell us to imitate Christ is because He lived and died as a genuine human being, was tempted like us in every respect, save without sin says the author of Hebrews. He was Adam gone right, starting the whole race over again with himself. Take some time to write down your reflections on this and questions about all of this. This is the season to contemplate the mystery of the Word took on flesh in the womb of Mary.

Fifty-second Sunday of the Year

9/26/71

"And being warned by God in a dream that they should not return to Herod, they departed into their own country by another way."
—Matthew 2.12

Astrological scholars from Chaldea were making a pilgrimage to Bethlehem. Outside they were guided by a heavenly light, and within they were guided by a spiritual illumination. The searching question they asked in the capital, Jerusalem, was, "Where is he born the King of the Jews?"—not the king of their own country. The search for the Christ transcends nationalism. They reached the manger, saw the child, presented their gifts and were ready to return. Being inwardly warned, they traveled back another way. They had an instinct that warned them about peril and they had a vision of the messiah. The "other way" was a new way. They had never traveled that way before.

The New Testament places an especial emphasis on the word "new." A Christian is a man on a new road. All things are new to such a person. Being new, it is a different way. The wise men went back to their own country by a different route. The river of time changed its course with that event in Bethlehem. But it was not just the wise men that went home by a different way. The story tells us that the holy family went home by way of Egypt, hardly the direct way to Nazareth! But that way was the safe way. Wise men included Joseph who protected the life of a little child by going home the other way. All of these men escaped the wrath of Herod by doing so. Finally, it was a homeward way, not just any other way. This other way led them home where they had an opportunity to rehearse their rich and surprising experiences again and again. Ever since then the vision of Christ has caused countless millions to go home another way. Are you walking that way for Christ? Do you know where home is?

During the holidays as we enjoyed the beautiful Christmas trees and their decorations, I wonder how many of us visualized the *true* Christmas tree—the old rugged cross, and its meaning? It was not decorated with flashy ornaments, but it was on that gruesome cross that the Prince of Peace died. He was the creator, and yet it was on that cross that He gave His life. The Bible says that while we were yet sinners, Christ died for our sins.

As we think about the birth of Jesus, let us turn our thoughts from the commercial Christmas tree and realize that Jesus was truly born to die on a rugged tree. As we look at the cross, we are directed to the only source of everlasting life. It is in and through Him alone that we find the forgiveness of our sins and the way to life now and hereafter. We can also see the horror of sin and its effects. We can see the price God paid, for we are not redeemed with corruptible things like silver and gold or by tradition, but by the precious blood of Jesus, who was guilty of no sin.

The cross divided the crowd at the crucifixion into two groups, the saved and the unsaved. The soldiers were callous, in the crowd there were rebels, and the religious leaders thought Jesus was a troublemaker. Even today, many religious leaders in many countries will reject Jesus as King of Kings and Lord of Lords. But those who come to the cross receive life now and everlasting life hereafter. The cross truly divides humanity.

We are no longer bond servants to sin, but rather heirs of God through Christ Jesus. Jesus has gone ahead to prepare a place for us and He said He will come again and receive us unto Himself and there will be no more sin, for the former things have passed away. The true Christmas tree was on a hill the shape of a skull, and on that tree hung the world's greatest love gift—God's provision, God's life, God's salvation.

I pray that as we saw the sparkle of the Christmas tree, we also saw the gleam of the tears in the eyes of Jesus. Then let us cling to that old rugged cross in a new way, redirecting our lives anew to His service, who gave up His life that we might have life everlasting.

12/29/68

Time marches on, another year has passed, a New Year soon begins. A poet once wrote "what is time"—the shadow on a sundial, the striking of a clock, the hourglass with its sifting sands? But no, these are only measurements of time. The Bible teaches that time and life are tied together, but sometimes it seems the whole world is organized for measuring time. Time is many things to different people. To the Christian time has a moral significance, we are to "redeem the time," but what does that really mean?

As life goes on billions of events are happening every moment of historic time and each person contributes his quota. What contribution have we made and do we hope to make? Time is neither good nor bad except as we make it so. Time has been given to us to glorify God, and to stay in contact with Him. It makes no difference how famous, how wealthy, or how much contribution you have made to literature or science the vital question is, have you glorified God by having that conversion experience to Christ? If not, you have lived at least partly in vain.

Time becomes an appointment. How are you bearing up with the test of time? How does it affect you? Are you growing daily in the grace and the knowledge of our Lord? Do you take advantage of every opportunity to study the Scriptures and to pray, to witness for Christ? As the world moves from crisis to crisis there will come another moment on God's clock. It will mean the end of this world's evil and the beginning of God's reign throughout the world. But wait—what really has made the difference so that we might now see time in the light of eternity? We need to see it in the light that shone on Golgotha.

Questions and Thoughts for Reflection

1. The Magi were astrologers in the sense of ancient stargazers. They were not like modern readers of the zodiac. The Magi were not kings, but astrologers were definitely in royal courts as consultants. So we

can stop singing "We Three Kings" now. We don't even know if there were three of them. That's a guess based on the number of gifts they brought. One of the more important things about their story is that the one God of the Bible was giving them guidance both externally and internally to go and find the child born to be King of the Jews. Sometimes Christians' visions of how God works are too narrow, as if He only uses pious Jews or Christians to reveal His will. This story makes clear that's false. We could also point to the story of a pagan prophet named Balaam, whom God used to bless Israel. Or more recently there is the impressive accounts of Jesus revealing Himself in dreams and visions to Muslims who have no contact with the Bible or Christian missionaries and have not been watching Christian things on the internet. The title of the book is *Dreams and Visions* by Tom Doyle and Greg Webster. It turns out God can reveal Himself to all sorts of people, including people who come from countries which have no Jewish or Christian presence to speak of. Is your vision of how God works too small and too narrow? God can reach people in all sorts of ways.

But it was not just the Magi, it was also the holy family that went home by another way involving a stay in Egypt until Herod the Great was off the scene. It seems to be often the case that God's people have to take a circuitous route to get home—consider also the wilderness wandering generation whose story is told in the Pentateuch. God often does things in what we would call irregular or abnormal ways with all sorts of irregular and unexpected people, which of course also characterizes the people Jesus chose to be among the Twelve. While God is reliable and unchanging, from a human point of view His actions are often unpredictable. There is a wonderful Christmas song by James Taylor called "Home by Another Way" about the wise men that is well worth a listen. It too emphasizes the mysteries of how God works.

One of the striking images in the first lesson for today is the notion that the cross is the real Christmas tree, the real tree that tells the story of human redemption. I agree with this. And my grandfather is right that the cross divides humanity in various ways. I recently heard a story about a stewardess on a British airlines plane who was a Christian and was asked to take off her cross, as it might offend someone. They were of course right; it does offend some people. As Paul says the cross is folly to some and a stumbling block to others. The stewardess refused to take off her cross. You know something has gone terrible wrong when a country that still has a Queen who is "the Defender of the Christian faith" and allows all sorts of bizarre and aberrant religious practices at Stonehenge and elsewhere has the nerve to ask a stewardess on a national airline to take off her cross. What's wrong with this picture?

2. In our last lesson in this study, we have the reflections of my grandfather on the cusp of a New Year. It is an interesting reflection on time, and the measurement of time. And he is right, as usual, that we seem, perhaps especially at the end of the year, all too preoccupied with the measurement and passage of time, rather than with redeeming the time and doing something Christian with it. Sometimes we can't even count right. Every century from the time of Jesus begins with the year 1, and ends with the year 100. This means that the change from 1999 to 2000 did *not* bring the dawn of a new century. That began on January 1, 2001. Surely, we can count from 1 to a hundred.

Sometimes, we talk about "passing the test of time" or "the right time" or "the opportune time" or that something is "about time" or "someone's time has come" and many more such phrases. We seem to be obsessed with time. Meanwhile, time marches on and we seem to be getting more done, less quickly. We live with constant distractions from making the most of our time, and making the main thing the main thing. I was recently asked why I didn't have one of these fancy new Apple watches which on a miniscule screen one can see emails, and even receive and send phone calls and texts. But frankly I don't want a watch that runs and ruins my day. I don't want to have to continually answer things on my watch! Mick Jagger was right to complain long ago about "the useless information supposed to fire my imagination, but I can't get no—satisfaction." What the information and technology age has done has shortened our attention spans, and made us much easier to distract from the main things we should be focusing on.

Hopefully, some of the thoughts in these studies have been timely for you, but as an exercise here at the end of the year I would suggest you chart how you spend your time each day for a whole week. Not a week of vacation, but a normal work week. I think you will find that some of us have too much leisure time on our hands, some too much work time on our hands, and almost all of us not enough worship and Scripture study and prayer time. Under these circumstances the increasing Biblical illiteracy of our culture, and the declining attendance at church in many, perhaps most, denominations these days is no surprise. There is a difference between being busy and being about God's business, between being productive and asking whether the products we are making or selling or buying are even worth having or can advance our relationships with God and others. Our priorities are often askew, and our devices while allowing more communication are at the same time dividing us. We need actual face time, not merely the app FaceTime. You can't embrace someone through the phone or computer. Think about these things as the New Year dawns.

Postscript

It was a cold February day in 1988, and I had had to fly in to Wilmington from Cleveland, as at the time I was teaching at Ashland Seminary in Ashland Ohio. My grandfather had died at ninety-two, and I was asked to do the homily on Romans 8, one of Pop's favorite passages. Little was I to know that in his Sunday school lessons he frequently cited "God works all things together for good for those who love God." The service went on for a while and then we rode out to the cemetery for his burial. I had not seen my grandfather in a long time as he was too old to visit us in Ohio, and we had been there since 1984. So, when we got to the graveside, I asked them to open just the head part of the casket so I could say goodbye. I leaned over and kissed him on the forehead and said "Goodbye, Pop," but later I realized I should have said, "I'll see you at home." As much as he used to talk about our eternal home in heaven in his lessons, that's what I should have said.

James Arthur West was a faithful Christian person unto death, and he still is. I do not know if I would be a teacher of the New Testament were it not for his encouragement to go to seminary and then go on and do doctoral work. The story has it that he also told my mother to not insist on my coming back to North Carolina to be a preacher after seminary. He knew there was a calling on my life and it required more education. And this from a man who was never able to go to college, not least because he had to support his brother and his family through some of the hard times during the early twentieth century. When it came to the Bible, he was self-educated, church-education, and Holy Spirit-educated. And he pursued that education with a passion. I have his old Bible and you can tell which parts he spent the most time in. Besides the New Testament it was clearly the Psalms.

I hope you have found these lessons or devotions helpful and that they encouraged you to dig into God's Word again and again. Pop had memorized various portions of Scripture, and here is a bit from Psalm 119 that he repeated regularly. May it be our cry as well.

> Your word is a lamp for my feet,
> a light on my path.
> I have taken an oath and confirmed it,
> that I will follow your righteous laws.
> I have suffered much;
> preserve my life, LORD, according to your word.
> Accept, LORD, the willing praise of my mouth,
> and teach me your laws.
> Though I constantly take my life in my hands,
> I will not forget your law.
> The wicked have set a snare for me,
> but I have not strayed from your precepts.
> Your statutes are my heritage forever;
> they are the joy of my heart.
> My heart is set on keeping your decrees
> to the very end.

www.ingramcontent.com/pod-product-compliance
Lightning Source LLC
Chambersburg PA
CBHW060833190426
43197CB00039B/2576